ROMANCE... PUSH THE ON BUTTON!

Romance... Push The On Button!

HOW TO TURN YOUR MAN INTO A ROMANTIC

Paul Gaughan

Contents

INTRODUCTION   1
1. CHAPTER ONE   3
2. CHAPTER TWO   21
3. CHAPTER THREE   30
4. CHAPTER FOUR   38
5. CHAPTER FIVE   59
6. CHAPTER SIX   75
7. CHAPTER SEVEN   97
8. CHAPTER EIGHT   125
9. CHAPTER NINE   182
10. CHAPTER TEN   208
11. CHAPTER ELEVEN   231
12. References   270

Dedication

To Sue

The one unique woman who taught me what real love was all about. My life has never been the same since you entered it. Although we have been together for years we never were able to leave the honeymoon period. Each day with you is a precious gift. Whenever you walk into a room I still can't take my eyes off you. I just have to lock eyes with you and I'm gone. It's impossible for me to ever be bored with you in my life. Let's keep pushing that button and see where it takes us next!

Copyright © 2020 by Paul Gaughan

All rights reserved. No part of this book may be reproduced in any manner whatsoever without written permission except in the case of brief quotations embodied in critical articles and reviews.

First Printing, 2020

INTRODUCTION

Your heartbeat races, the rest of the world fades out of focus as your eyes meet his. You feel desire welling up within your body, and he is just so gorgeous you want him to take hold of you and kiss you all night long. If only you could freeze this moment in time, and the two of you could be like this forever. But is it like that now? Don't you want it to be? As you look at your man today, is he the same as when you first fell in love, or does he seem so different..., so boring..., so... unromantic?

Well take heart because this book is for you. You can experience the exhilaration and excitement again of romance if you are prepared to carry out the principles you are about to read. Make sure you read the whole book first though, so you can get the total picture. Romance is not just for the first year of a relationship. Romance is meant to be forever.

When you think about it, every woman wishes to change some things about her man. In fact, many women often view their men before a long term relationship as what they can change them into. The important point to realise in turning your partner into a romantic, is not so much the importance of it being your desire, but it being his desire once he can see its benefits. It is persuading him to give it a go - what has he possibly got to lose? It is getting him to experience being a romantic and letting him get addicted to the idea. It is teaching him there are incredible benefits for him that he has never before understood or even considered.

It's like tasting a new food for the first time. Some people don't try it because they don't like the look of it. Then they miss out. Others talk themselves into not liking it - trying it but having their minds made up beforehand so as to ensure they will not like it and will not give it a fair trial. What this book does is it shows you what you need to do to allow your man to give true romance an honest try, and let him see how beneficial romance is for you both. It will give you lots of tools to change that man of yours into what he should be, what he may once or never has been, a real romantic. Then you will also read how to keep him that way; keep him addicted to romance for the rest of your lives. Oh, and one last thing, I hope your blood pressure's up to it!

1

CHAPTER ONE

ROMANCE AND THE CAVEMAN

"What is it with you and the caveman thing?" she asked. "And why, oh why, do I like it so much?" (Jill Shalvis, The Sweetest Thing)

How romantic was the ancient caveman? Well if you believe many people's imagination of what it was like, you would probably come up with an image of a caveman, club in hand dragging his woman by the hair behind him and that was about as romantic as it got! Whatever your prehistoric images, it does help to understand some of the basic concepts of primitive society to comprehend where we are today. So what are some of the things we are sure about the past that have ingrained themselves in our DNA even to the present day? One thing is certain, and that is that historically man was the hunter.

CAVEMAN CHARACTERISTIC 1
Man The Hunter
Dominant Sense - Sight

It was the man's traditional role to track and hunt game for the table, provide shelter and ward off any threat to his family. In other words, man was to provide for the physical needs, the basics, the most important things if he was to survive. The priorities were to kill the wild beast, remove any threat (including any other man that wanted to steal his woman away from him) and be totally self-reliant. This incredibly physical world required one important thing from a man - testosterone, and lots of it! Of his five senses his primary sense was sight. This was used to track and trap animals, make weapons and tools, and find water, food and shelter. When he was confronted with a challenge or stressful situation, his testosterone, adrenaline and muscles always provided an answer. He could fight or run. Most of all he felt needed. He felt in charge.

Corresponding Trait Today's Woman Wants

Confidence is one of the single most traits that attracts women today. Sure it comes in various forms but whether it be the "bad boy", the "show off", or at times the little bit "cocky adventurer", all these different types are an evolution from the hunter caveman. A man who overflows with confidence, knows where he is going, is a natural leader rather than a follower, and knows how to take charge can be attractive qualities in a man that grabs the attention of women. If a man knows what he is about and clearly possesses confidence then a women has a lower risk of facing an uncertain future with such a man. That is why he can be so alluring to her.

So what has changed after so many years? Has the basic make-up of a man changed, or just the environment in which he now finds himself? Well adrenaline still cuts in under stress to ready a man for a fight or flight response. Testosterone still seems to ooze from a man's pores and he has lost none of his competitive nature or abilities to deal with physical challenges. But his environment has changed radically, and man's traditional role has become extinct. Man is no longer needed to provide the basic necessities of life. There's no threatening beast to kill, no game to hunt and no cave to claim. The main challenges now are balancing the budget, paying the mortgage, and endless bills, perhaps getting reports in on time at work, and being a sensitive new age guy all from behind a desk rather than out in the jungle. What good is testosterone for these modern day challenges? The answer is that it is not much good at all. In fact it can be a downright disadvantage at times. In addition, a man knows deep down that he is no longer needed or totally depended on as his woman is now capable of earning her own living, if she wants to and quite often does. Man's role in reproduction is also now no longer essential with IVF therapy and the brave new world of cloning also presenting further possibilities of man's redundancy. Has man himself become a dinosaur?

Even some governments seek to undermine a man's traditional role by making sure that if a man loses his job, the government will step in with unemployment payments to take care of the basic, physical necessities. So, many a man feeling obsolete and no longer needed or appreciated sits at home unemployed and loses his self-esteem, dignity and identity quicker than any other way. This can be why problems associated with the security of a man's work affect him so intensely.

How Today's Man Gets It So Wrong - Control

The hunter/provider today is losing confidence. But the negative trait driven by fear that often takes its place is control. Man for thousands of years has been using his physical strength and size to control women. But women are sick of being controlled by men. A man today is often not the only hunter-gatherer-provider of his family unit. He is now often confusing confidence with being in charge so much that he is controlling. Today we witness in society men who continue to shock with domestic violence. Often these men are unable to gain power in their lives. They are unable to earn respect, they no longer can win a fight with a savage beast and show their mastery to the world and so they end up fighting with the women in their lives and try to gain physical ascendancy over an easier target. It may not be so overt as domestic violence. It could be far more subtle as a man trying to gain financial control over his partner. It may be him wanting to win every single argument he ever has with her. It might be him unable to ever admit he is wrong. It might be wanting to control how his partner acts, what she wears or who she spends her time with. But it is controlling still the same. This shadow side of confidence, this morphed version of confidence is also so strong at times women are still attracted by it. Often women who grow up in abusive homes still become attracted to further abuse because it is what they are familiar with, it is what they are used to and it seems like a sense of what home was like. So much so that women who have been in abusive relationships often stay in them. They seem to always believe what their abusive partner tells them, that he has changed or that he won't hit her again.

As well as control the main problem in relation to romance and women is that a man still tries to live like a caveman, a hunter and gatherer in certain ways. The man still places great importance on the physical aspect of the relationship. **Sight is still his primary sense.**

This dominant sense of sight has pervaded the whole of modern society. Women are so sensitive to it that millions now suffer from body image issues. No one can escape looking at near naked female bodies. Whether it is in advertisements, the news, dress or the latest Instagram sensation. Women have bought right into it as well.

But while a modern day man is being constantly bombarded by images designed to catch his attention he is still all at sea with how to use his DNA to being a great partner to the modern woman in his life. Being a SNAG (Sensitive New Age Guy) just doesn't come naturally with all that testosterone. Many men still believe they are good partners if they only provide the basic, physical necessities in the relationship. If they work hard and long hours they expect that will meet their partner's needs and prove to their partners that they love them.

> *Many men still believe they are good partners if they only provide the basic, physical necessities in the relationship.*

Today the caveman's response is still to control by solving the problem, stopping the crying, and not showing any emotion or weakness. He believes he is successful in intimate relationships if he can stop any threat or is good at anything physical in the relationship. Yes, there probably is still a little bit of caveman left in every man. Or is it more than a *little* bit? At the end of the day a man is a man and that creature is very different from a woman!

CAVEMAN CHARACTERISTIC 2
Lacking In Communication Skills – Often Struggles With Emotional Depth

If we think of an ancient caveman's linguistic skills we might think of him being limited to grunts. Much like teenage boys as they progress through that terrible, awkward stage before they arrive at manhood.

There wasn't much need to talk when the caveman was on the hunt. He was used to being a lone wolf creeping through the wild, sneaking up on game. He was focused on getting things done, not talking about them.

Corresponding Trait Today's Woman Is Drawn To

Women still get curious about the tall, strong silent types. They want to get in under his skin and find out what he is like deep down. They are often drawn to the challenge a quiet man presents. It is as if they want him to be quiet to everyone else but open up to them. They are drawn to the challenge of being able to congratulate themselves once they can connect with him down at a deeper level. Women bond through speech. They love to connect through speaking. Many a woman has fell in love with a man's voice. That deep, very masculine confident voice can be an extreme turn on. The other thing that a woman is drawn to about the caveman is that he is a good listener. He doesn't dominate the conversation. He can allow her to speak and even if he is drifting off somewhere else in his mind he can look like he is listening! The problem is however, that many of these quiet types are exactly like that – very, very quiet.

How Today's Man Gets It So Wrong

Many men still struggle with communication skills. Whether it is becoming defensive way too quickly, struggling to cope with depth or just opening up to a greater depth emotionally. Often men are singled focused. So even when they are home, their mind can still be stuck on the hunt. Whether today that means their minds are still stuck on work or on their hobby, many men struggle to converse on an intimate level with the woman in their life. A modern man can tell stories from his own modern day hunt. He can relay facts. He can tell his partner how to fix things. He can make tools, explain mechanics and how to use things. But can he connect at an emotional level? Can he talk about himself and can he actually enjoy deep and meaningful long conversations with his woman? Can he be right at home being in touch and expressing his emotions to her? This is where a man can get it so wrong. He can be so focused on other things, he leaves his partner emotionally alone.

Years ago John Powell came up with the levels of communication. I referred to it in my first book where I wanted to make men aware of how important it is to be able to communicate at deeper levels in their communication with women. Powell's five levels are simply,

Level 1 Cliché Conversations
Level 2 Reporting facts
Level 3 Ideas or judgements
Level 4 Feelings and emotions
Level 5 Complete personal commitment[1]

The deepest level is where communication is deep but both get the other perfectly! There is this magical connection where everything seems just perfect and the positive emotions are being generated just by being in the other's presence. The point I wish to make here is that to get to the deepest level a person has to firstly master level 4. Men usually have no trouble with the first three but often stumble at level 4. But men who can communicate at level 5 with ease are the ones who have a high intimacy tolerance. They can easily tolerate and even enjoy long conversations of depth with the woman in their lives. This high intimacy tolerance in a man can be an extremely romantic trait for a woman to see in a man. In fact many a woman is constantly searching for it in her hunt for a partner. For the quiet caveman who only grunts, she is hoping "still waters run deep" and she will be able to plumb his depths and connect with him at level 5 on a constant basis.

CAVEMAN CHARACTERISTIC 3
Is Strong – Can Keep The Wolves Away
Dominant Feature – Strength and Muscles

The caveman was the protector. He was the strong man who kept his family safe. No one would mess with him which made his family feel safe. To be in the wild by herself a woman could feel at the mercy of the wild and the elements but not with the caveman by her side to take care of business. She could feel safe under his protection. The caveman had to work out. He had to fight to stay alive. He loved being strong and muscular. He loved seeing off any threat.

Corresponding Trait Today's Woman Is Drawn To – Security

Today's woman wants to feel safe with her man. No, there's nothing wrong with muscles in her modern man. But a woman needs more. She's not only looking for a tall, physically strong man. She wants one who is going to lower her anxiety. She wants a man who is going to hang around. She wants to feel safe in the relationship. This means a man who is not afraid to commit to being with her for ever. Such a man grounds her when she becomes emotional and she doesn't even understand herself. Such a man keeps her calm and secure. Such a man is one that will never abandon her or leave her to the wild. She could survive on her own. But why would she want to? Life is hard enough. When a woman knows her man is never going to abandon her, she faces the world from a secure position. She is content when she has that secure connection with her mate. When she can connect with him and knows that connection is as strong as steel, she can relax to take on other challenges without unease. She is content, secure and free of anxiety.

How Today's Man Gets It So Wrong

A man today might overly focus on his physical physique at the expense of developing in other areas. But while there is nothing wrong with a man being strong and muscular, many modern men get it wrong by being a strong island. A man can be so focused on him being strong he will never ask for any help. He thinks he must do everything by himself in order for him to see himself as strong. This self-subsistence attitude is a huge problem in men's health. This having to rely on others really irritates the modern day caveman. Whether he gets symptoms of prostate cancer or even a heart attack, he tends to think he will be all right by himself. He tends to minimise the symptoms and puts off seeking expert medical help. This too tough to care attitude kills many a man who, if he would have sought medical help when the symptoms first appeared, would still be alive today. A modern day caveman also gets it wrong by not letting his woman inside. He believes he has to be so tough that he can never be vulnerable. But it makes him a lone wolf emotionally and not a team player. He often likes preserving his rough exterior giving the illusion the inside is the same. He makes the mistake of being unable to be vulnerable and connect with his partner at a deep level. He settles for a shallow intimacy tolerance and he never experiences the rewards of going deeper with her. He sometimes wants to be strong and be the leader and so it stops him from truly connecting and allowing the beauty of joint leadership.

The Cave Woman

There have been some tremendous changes for women in the last several decades in relation to women's roles, feminism, equality issues and the entering of women into what once were exclusively, traditional male occupations. But these changes have only increased the vulnerability of the male ego. Independence for women has meant that the caveman characteristics are needed far less than before. Furthermore, women have only added to their role rather than turning it completely on its head like the caveman's role. You see the traditional abilities and roles of the cave woman are still inherently active in today's society.

> ***Women have only added to their role rather than turning it completely on its head like the caveman's role.***

What was the cave woman like? She was the nurturer, the care giver, the supporter. She cared for the vulnerable and for those who couldn't care for themselves. She nursed babies, raised the family and cared for her caveman's needs so he could be strong and go out and hunt. **Her primary sense was hearing**. She could hear her baby cry and could instinctively understand immediately what her baby was communicating. For the caveman, a cry was a cry; all he wanted to do was to solve the problem which to him was to stop the crying. But the cave woman knew the difference between a painful cry, a hunger cry, a "Change my nappy cry" and an, "I'm just being naughty cry"! So incredible where her powers of hearing and communicating.

The cave woman looked up to her caveman and felt secure in his tower of strength, his testosterone, his ruggedness and how he would provide for their needs. Her soft skin and gentler ways made such a contrast to him, yet they both depended on each other. Each time he brought home the game to put on the table she would affirm him that he was a successful caveman. He loved that appreciation which made him try even harder to bring back bigger, more or better choice game for the table. She liked how rugged he was outside the cave but enjoyed the challenge of taming this wild beast inside the cave. She liked how he was rugged to everyone else but soft to her inside their cave. She loved it when he would tell of his adventures, his contests with beasts. She always had a vision and a dream of what the two of them could do together, and she constantly nurtured and gave of herself to their family as it grew. She always viewed her family as an extension of herself and their relationship.

Today women are still generally the primary nurturers. They still bear children and still know what a baby's cry means, much to the amazement of their partner. Although they may now have employment outside the home, they still raise a family, care for a large part of the house and for their man's needs as well. So yesterday's cave woman has become today's super woman because roles have only been added to women and stacked on top of each other instead of substituted.

> *Yesterday's cave woman has become today's super woman because roles have only been added to women and stacked on top of each other instead of substituted.*

Today's Cavemen and Women

Let's tie all this together concerning romance and emotional needs in intimate relationships, now that we have considered the caveman and the cave woman. A woman's primary sense is still hearing. She longs to hear the sound of her man's voice. She longs for him to communicate to her and nurture her by telling her of his undying love for her. No longer is there any game on the table to tell her how he loves her. No dragons to slay to show her that he would fight any wild creature just to come home to her (mind you battling the freeway can be just as tiring!). These romantic acts are no longer evident and so today's modern woman continues to search every day for evidence of her man's love and devotion. "Does he still believe I am special and appealing?" This she questions every time she wants him to respond to her communication. But it is such a difficult task to get this caveman who no longer hunts, to express his love for her. Slaying the dragon for the fair maiden and coming to her aid is no longer needed or always appreciated by today's independent woman. But there is one thing she does cry out for - romance, little expressions of love. Yet regretfully, romance is usually missing from so many long-term relationships. Those expressions of undying love, the man placing the game on the table, the communicating at a deeper level, his expression of love to her continually every day in a way she understands, all these are often missing from today's relationships.

A woman's emotional needs in her intimate relationship today still involve the following three areas:

1. **Confidence in their relationship and the future**
2. **Communication at a deeper level**
3. **Security – lack of anxiety**

These three things she needs more than anything else. But breakups are at an all time high. There is no time to merely sit around the fire and just simply talk. Today, many women and even men for that matter, spend more time interacting with and nurturing their social media accounts than they do with their intimate partner on a daily basis. Finally, anxiety disorders are the most common of all the mental health issues and are at higher rates than at any time previously in recorded history.

In long term relationships these three needs often go unanswered for years. The woman often doesn't know how to ask for them, and the man doesn't know they even exist, let alone how to fulfil them. The result is that so many relationships fall miles short of their potential because whenever needs are not met, negative emotions are generated and appear in all sorts of areas within the relationship.

Romance is the solution to a woman's needs in all three of these areas. Romance can make her confident in their relationship, communicate deeply to her the language of love and make her feel secure in her relationship with her man. Other chapters in this book explore getting this whole concept across to men. But why don't men instinctively understand women's needs or why don't men have a need themselves for feeling secure in the relationship like women do? The answer lies in the fundamental difference between how men and women view their intimate relationships and it has a lot to do with our cave dwelling ancestors.

Past Verses Present

In their intimate relationships men use the past as a guide to their relationship. To ascertain the health of their relationship, a man will reason from past experience and logic. When he was a caveman he used his past experience and logic to guide him to track animals. A knowledge of seasons would allow him to understand the migratory habits of his prey and the increase in needs of his family for warmth during winter and water during summer. He was used to doing things. Today is no exception. A man still thinks that he has to prove his love by logic and doing masculine things. His proof of his relationship is in the past. He reasons he has worked for years to provide for his family. He might even have a marriage certificate to prove he is married, therefore he is. His proof is a logical deduction from past, physical happenings.

The formula a man uses is like this. "We live together. We are intimate. Therefore all is well - we **must** love each other." The physical aspect is still so important to most men. If all is well financially and sexually, then the relationship is fine he thinks. Men reason, "Look at all the things I have done for you (in the *past*), therefore I love you, therefore you know it, therefore I don't have to tell you".

> *If all is well financially and sexually, then the relationship is fine he reasons.*

A Woman Lives in the Present

This thinking is the opposite to a woman's thinking because she instinctively operates on feelings instead of reasoning from the past as a man does. Feelings are always in the ***present***. How you feel now can be different from the past or the future. Present needs must be fulfilled now. Who wants to wait for the future or look to the past to fulfil a felt need? It is this basic difference that most men fail to understand or appreciate. No matter how big an effort was made years ago, it is the constant, little, ***present*** acts of affection and connection that a woman wants from her man. This is why it is the woman who is always asking, "Do you love me?" She wants to feel loved in the present, right now. Yesterday's romance is not enough for a woman. She wants devotion today, right now from her man. Who knows, things could have changed since yesterday, and how would she know any different? She feels this way regardless of how good yesterday was. "Do I feel loved now? Where are the signs now in the present that tell me what my man thinks of me?", she wonders.

> *This is why it is the woman who is always asking, "Do you love me?" She wants to feel loved in the present, right now.*

Proof to a woman is not in the past, it has to be a ***present feeling***. The present always contains the following implicit questions for a woman in an intimate relationship:

"What are my present needs?"

"Does my man want to meet my emotional needs?"

"What is he thinking right now?"

"How does he feel towards me now?"

"Does he love me now?"

"Will he show me that he loves me now (with acts of affection and connection)?"

Proof to a woman is not in the past, it has to be a present feeling.

Her formulae is the opposite sequence of his. She reasons, "If there are plenty of signs in the present that we love each other, then yes, we are intimate, we are connected, and we do have a loving relationship." As far as the physical dimension is concerned, she reasons, "If the relationship is good, this allows me to get more out of the sexual side." A romantic, connected relationship increases the physical enjoyment for her so that she gets more out of intimacy.

Bringing the Two Together

This past verses present turmoil builds conflict as a woman's needs are not fulfilled, the man does not feel appreciated and the physical side of the relationship goes downhill. Where did all the passion go they both wonder? It is only when both partners understand where the other is coming from that it all begins to make sense. When he starts to fulfil her needs in the present, to be loved, cherished, romanced, and connected emotionally, she begins to appreciate him more and more. She becomes aroused physically to him and barriers in their relationship melt away. All because they both understand the different perspectives of past verses present.

It is only when both partners understand where the other is coming from that it all begins to make sense.

A man who doesn't understand this thinks that he has to give up his caveman status, all of his testosterone and masculinity, if he has to become romantic and start to communicate his feelings to the woman he loves. He thinks he has to give up being a virile man and become an effeminate eunuch in order to be a romantic. But a man who understands the differences between men and women (in regards to past verses present, differing needs and thinking) understands that romance is indeed very masculine. In her eyes more romance, more emotional connection, more developing of deeper bonds, means he is more masculine because it shows her he loves her, she feels loved, and her needs are fulfilled. Romance makes her want to give her all, it turns her on and makes her feel more feminine. It inspires her to meet her partner's needs like never before and both find the fires of passion become self-perpetuating. The relationship grows even better with the passing of time as the former formulae of "meet my needs", is replaced with, "meet each other's unique needs."

Now that we have looked at the caveman DNA and how it works against men in this modern age we are going to explore how romance is the answer to bringing men and women together into a secure place of pleasure. Romance is so important because it meets all of those desires and needs that a woman longs for in her intimate relationship. We will also look further at what romance is, why it is so important, how to communicate your needs (including romantic needs) to your mate, how a man can best meet those needs, and how easy it can be for him. You will then learn how to destroy the myths men have about romance, how to educate your man about romance, how to convince men of the importance of romance and lots of different ways and ideas to inject romance into your life. We will also discover how to let pleasure into your life because romance brings lots of pleasure with it. Then we will finally discover how to truly connect deeply with your partner.

SUMMARY OF CHAPTER ONE

The Caveman Was:

1. **The Hunter**
   Dominant sense – sight
   The corresponding trait that women desire in today's caveman is confidence.
   Men get confidence wrong by turning it into control. Men get focused on providing the physical necessities in the relationship and wanting to win rather than connect.
2. **Lacking in communication skills and struggles with emotional depth**
   The corresponding trait that women desire in today's caveman is a manly voice and a challenge to plumb the man's depths.
   Men get it wrong by not mastering deeper levels of communication, tuning out and having a low intimacy tolerance.
3. **Strong – he knew how to keep threats away**

The corresponding trait that women desire in today's caveman is feeling safe and secure.
Man gets it wrong by being an island and not being vulnerable with her.
The Cave Woman Was a Nurturer.

Dominant sense - hearing.
She still looks for:
Confidence in their relationship
Communication at a deeper level
Security and lack of anxiety
Romance can be the answer which meets all of a woman's needs in one place.
A man argues from past logic to arrive at a present conclusion.
A woman lives and feels in the present because feelings are always in the present.
This is why a woman is always seeking, "Do you love me?"
Romance brings the past, present and future together to restore the pleasure back into relationships.

2

CHAPTER TWO

THE ELEMENTS OF ROMANCE

"You know you're in love when you can't fall asleep because reality is finally better than your dreams." (Dr Seuss)

When I first began researching for this book I thought I would find volumes on romance. I was amazed though to find a dearth on such an important topic. In fact, many libraries' computer files showed nothing relevant at all under the subject of romance in the **non**-fiction section! (Most entries under romance were on romantic **music**!) As I gathered together and hungrily consumed any material on the subject I came across a strong current of opposition towards romance in general. Articles, often written by men, seemed to cast aside romance as being unrealistic, only fanciful and for immature lovers. Kenneth N. Anderson and Robert M. Goldenson state this general feeling towards romance in, *The Language of Sex from A to Z World Almanac* p 216 where they write the entry under "*Romantic Love*". "Romantic love is a highly emotional, starry-eyed relationship based largely on idealisation, physical attraction, adoration, and a large dash of fantasy - but it usually ignores practical, down to earth realities of life."[2]

This may be the cold interpretation of romance that many have, but it is certainly not shared by myself. I would like to offer you a totally different view of romance. Especially different in my view is that great romance *is* achievable in reality. Romance is not something just confined to the pages of fairy tales and fantasy but it can take place in your own, real life. True, the realities of life cannot be substituted for constant romance but romance can be added to them, to break them up and make them fulfilling. It may to some degree depend upon your definition of romance but I believe that every intimate relationship can benefit from the addition of romantic gestures. So remember, regardless of what anyone tells you, romance is achievable in *your* relationship and all relationships can move onto a higher romantic level under certain conditions.

Every intimate relationship can benefit from the addition of romantic gestures.

The only exception of course is if you have a totally unrealistic concept of romance. So what exactly is the definition of romance? Romance is very hard to define. It goes beyond a dictionary meaning in ink and words. Romance is something you have to feel, something you have to experience to know what I mean, but once experienced there seems no substitute and no language to explain it. Although difficult to put into words I would like to offer my own definitions of romance.

You won't find these in a dictionary but they do convey a positive idea of romance that express its different aspects.

Romance is:

-unpredictably expressing love in different ways and at different times.

-when the man you love, loves you with all of himself and constantly shows you in new and exciting ways.

-when a man gets a woman to want him, and I mean really want him. It is driving her crazy with desire for him. Any action that enhances this desire in her for him can be considered romantic. (If this is true then individual romantic gestures can be a matter of individual taste. Just like music, what one person considers great may be average for another.)

-when your lover does exactly what you want him to do without him being told or even given a hint. Great romance is when he surprises you with something really exciting and lovable that you haven't even thought of yourself.

-using a love tool (a candlelit dinner, a beautifully presented bunch of flowers, a special thought, a surprise or gift, a personally written love poem, etc.) in such a way that all your inhibitions are lowered and you melt all over, becoming warm dough, trusting in his sculpturing hands.

-the art of making someone fall in love with you.

- to be treated as if you were the most attractive, indeed the only woman in the world.

- the art of keeping someone madly in love with you.

- the art of having someone grow in their love for you.

- being there to listen intently to you, whenever you need to share, and just makes you feel totally connected.

To define romance for yourself is one thing but to get those concepts across to your man is another. Unfortunately, as Dr James Dobson explains in his book, ***What Wives Wish Their Husbands Knew About***

Women, "Women often find it impossible to convey their needs for romantic affection to their husbands"[3]. Why is this so? Perhaps there are many answers but one is surely because of the fact that romance, in order to be true romance, must be initiated by the male. It has to be his attitude, his idea. Otherwise it just falls flat. Another reason is no doubt the fear of being misunderstood, being made fun of or not taken seriously.

But whatever reason you may have, you must come to the point of realising the importance of your man being aware of your romantic needs even if it does mean for you to take the initiative the first time. Sometimes men just have no **practical** understanding and although it may be hard for you, some men do need it spelled out for them. One way of helping a man understand what romance is, is by telling him what romance is **not**.

Some men do need it spelled out for them.

Tracy Cabot in her book gives a terrific list on what's romantic and what's not. She even recommends tearing out the page and giving it to your partner. Here is her list.

1. Being alone together, just the two of us, is romantic. Being with other people is not.
2. A wonderful, unexpected, extravagant gift is romantic. A new vacuum cleaner is not.
3. Flowers from the florist are romantic. Steaks from the meat market are not.
4. Eating out is romantic. Eating at home is not.
5. Fancy restaurants are romantic, cafeterias and buffets are not.
6. Walking in the park at sunset is romantic. Jogging at dawn is not.

7. Staying overnight at a hotel with room service is romantic. Motel 6 is not.
8. Long, ambling scenic drives are romantic. Rushing through traffic is not.
9. Staying at a country inn is romantic. Going on an incentive trip or to a convention is not.
10. Talking over breakfast is romantic. Reading the papers is not.
11. Fancy cocktails, fine wine and champagne are romantic. Beer is not.
12. Window shopping at Gucci's is romantic. Browsing at the auto supply store is not.
13. Being swept away is romantic. Stopping for gas is not.
14. Love letters are romantic. Reminder notes are not.
15. Looking through old photos is romantic. Sorting bills is not.
16. Art, the ballet, poetry are romantic. Boxing, off-road racing and *Playboy* magazine are not.
17. Old movies and love stories are romantic. Shoot-'em ups and horror flicks are not.
18. Going away is romantic. Taking the kids is not.
19. Surprises are romantic. The same old thing is not.
20. Soft music is romantic. Football and baseball games are not.
21. Telling me how good I look is romantic. Saying how good some other woman looks is not.[4]

This list also illustrates clearly that men must appreciate that it is *how* things are done that is important. The destination seems so important to men but they have to be taught the pleasures of enjoying the journey as well. This relates to romance, sex and life in general. So by educating your partner so that he knows what is romantic and what is not, you can help him to appreciate why this is so, and what romance really is all about. You will also notice in the above list that for it to be truly romantic, there can be no secondary reason for the activity. You can't kill two birds with one stone when romance is involved. For something to be truly romantic the gesture has to be its own goal. You can't just tuck a romantic angle onto something you have to do anyway and then call it romantic, it just doesn't work that way. Romance has to come first and be the sole reason for something to be genuinely romantic.

It is how things are done that is important.

Let's have a look at some other elements of romance so that we have a deeper understanding of romance. One of the best ways of learning what something is all about, is to see it operating **correctly**. Think about the most romantic couple you know. What secrets do they have that you can incorporate into your relationship? Study them and learn from them. I have compiled an analytical list of characteristics of romantic couples to see how romance operates in people's lives. We really have to consider a romantic **couple** because part of romance is sharing. It is togetherness. We don't generally think of a hermit being romantic - successful romantics are not lonely, others are always drawn to them.

The Characteristics of Successfully Romantic Couples

1. They are healthy. They look after themselves. They care for their bodies and are careful not to abuse their bodies because they know their partner would be hurt by such abuse. They plan to love for a long time. They don't purposely scar themselves or make themselves ugly.

2. They know how to use romantic acts and gestures to their full potential. They have an eye for detail and make sure no distraction will rob them of any desired effect.

3. They are in love and they know it - even if they deny it in the early stages of their relationship. Not only do they know it but also the whole world knows it. Everyone can't help being aware of the fact. There is no guesswork here because it is so obvious. Their relationship is the number one priority in their lives. It consumes them and they seem whole and happy only when they are together.

4. They seem to always have an abundant supply of energy when it comes to their relationship. They never seem too tired to be romantic, never too tired to go out on a date or to spend time kissing and being in love.

5. He brings out her femininity and she brings out his masculinity. They seem to be good for each other and feed off each other. When they are together their strengths are multiplied and their weaknesses are not so noticeable.

6. There is often an element of mystery and surprise in one or both characters. Not all the information is known about the other and it arouses curiosity and desire. There is unpredictability and spontaneity in their relationship.

7. They are never bored. Life is exciting to them because they have each other and their lives revolve around each other.

8. They have a seductive power over their partner. They know how to prolong foreplay and enjoy every stage of lovemaking for what it is and has to offer.

9. They know they are loved by their partner and are confident in that love. There are no doubts that continually plague them.

10. Both are demonstrative and expressive in their love for each other. Expressions of their love for each other isn't hard work, but flow freely. They are outgoing to each other, not reserved, inhibited or introverted. They feel right at home in each other's presence.

11. They are good communicators. Even without talking they seem to know what the other is thinking.

12. They meet their partner's needs as no one else can.

13. Even if one or both partners are an underdog they can overcome great odds to achieve their goals. They are successful in fulfilling their dreams.

14. They touch each other frequently. They are not starved of touch or hugs, neither are they cold or frigid. They are happy persons and love life. They are not sour-faced but attract people by their positive, optimistic outlook. Being happy and contented is romantic - sad and miserable isn't. Romantic lovers smile more. They are slow to criticise

and are generous to others, erring on the side of giving the other the benefit of the doubt rather than intolerance.

15. They know how to connect. They connect regularly and deeply.

Try and see what areas may be lacking in your own relationship in regard to the above list. What can *you* do to change yourself so that you are a romantic partner in your own relationship? Something that happens in a relationship is that you learn from your partner. When one leads the other often follows. Being as close to another as we are in long term relationships makes us incorporate different characteristics into our own psyche. So provide a romantic lead in your own relationship by modelling your living on what you think a romantic woman is like and does.

SUMMARY OF CHAPTER TWO

- Romance is achievable in reality - it doesn't have to be just fantasy.
- It is difficult to define romance in words, it is more a positive feeling to be experienced.
- Help your man to understand what romance is by explaining what's **not** romantic.
- Communicate to your mate that it is the *how* things are done that is important.
- Understand the characteristics of romantic couples so you can incorporate them into your own relationship.

3

CHAPTER THREE

WHY ROMANCE DIES IN LONG TERM RELATIONSHIPS

"Promise me you'll never forget me, because if I thought you would, I'd never leave." (A.A. Milne)

Romance - is there a word comparable to it in the English language? Once experienced to its full potential it is addictive and no substitute can equal its power. For those of us who have experienced this all-consuming, all conquering power of romance, which we wish so desperately to keep forever, it is an ugly blow if we suddenly realise the romantic flame has been extinguished.

Does romance ever last forever? What are the reasons for that subtle, insidious change from the raging passion of romance that colours everything we do and think, to the ho-hum routine with which most long term relationships seem inevitably destined? Let's have a brief look at the reasons why romance disappears, what you can do to turn that man of yours into a passionate, thoughtful romantic, and finally how to keep him like that for a life time.

Reasons Why Romance Doesn't Last

Although no one likes to admit it before their marriage, most people admit after just a few short years of married life that the romantic side of their relationship has had to give way to the "practical" side of living. Often young lovers believe theirs is a special kind of love that will remain romantic forever - but why do so few ever accomplish it?

The Candle

Let's liken a long term relationship to a candle, and imagine romance as its flickering flame. What are the physical ingredients necessary to keep that flame alight? Well first of all we need a spark to ignite the flame. Next we need the wax to provide the fuel for the flame and then the right conditions that include oxygen to keep the flame burning.

We have to assume that there is some spark in your relationship to begin with, some spark that attracted you initially. It's always good to actually spend time talking together about the initial spark that ignited the passion between you and your man. The main ingredients however, the fuel and the conditions, need to be continuously supplied. You see, in many relationships the flame of romance goes out because the wax melts and is not replaced. It runs out of fuel because no fuel is added to the fire. The candle you ignited when you first got together does not contain enough fuel to burn for the next fifty or so years.

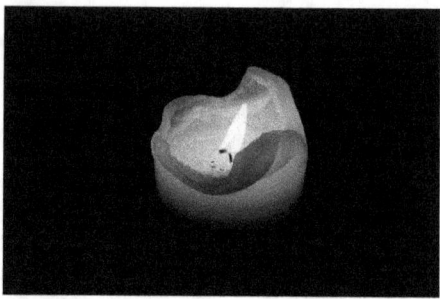

The candle you ignited when you first got together does not contain enough fuel to burn for the next fifty or so years.

Many couples wonder why their relationship no longer burns with the power of a steam train. But when they first hopped aboard their steam train journey they were shovelling in buckets of coal to produce that power and passion. Later on in this book we will look in detail at how to provide this fuel for romance. We will also look at how you can provide the right conditions for this flame, so that the flame will burn brightly without suffocation or running out of fuel.

Newness

When your relationship was new and exciting it was provided with change all the time. There were all sorts of new places, new dates, and new things to discover about your mate. Your whole relationship was characterised by a few words, but most of all it was "new". New things intrigue us all, feed our curiosity inviting us to accept the challenge of exploration, with the possibility of the fulfilment of all our dreams. We become positive in our expectations by asking, "Could this be what I am looking for? Am I in love with Prince Charming?" Our emotions shoot from a snail's pace to the freeway fast lane as we give of ourselves, and as we commit a little more we are confronted with both the threat and excitement of self-exposure to our new companion.

But that is now no longer the scenario. Now after years of being together, newness has been substituted for routine. No longer do you go out together on dates regularly. Why? Perhaps for many couples the reason, although never verbalised to each other, is this: When you were dating you went out on dates **to be together**. He lived at his place, you lived at yours and so you went out to be together. However, now that you are together all of the time your partner may reason, "Why waste money going out just to be together?" So gradually the candle runs out of fuel and the newness that you both wanted to last forever gradually morphs into the boring practicalities of a long term relationship life.

Pseudo Togetherness

Added to this lack of dates is the illusion that living together means sharing and being together in every sense of the word. Two people can start living together but if they don't have "quality time" shared together, they can become just flatmates. Before you were living together not only were there probably plenty of dates but there were those times when you talked about and shared your values, your dreams and the things that really count in your life. The conditions were created for that expression, that opening up, that understanding and acceptance of each other; something that is so important but so often seems to get pushed to the side as your life together ages.

Two people can start living together but if they don't have "quality time" shared together, they can become just flatmates.

Idiosyncrasies

In addition to all of this, after a few years of being together we seem to be more aware of our partners' bad points. Those little things we never even noticed before under the romantic candlelight have now been amplified under the magnifying glass of marital broad daylight. Before, or in the early days of our relationship, we didn't realise he picked his nose so much, didn't lower the toilet seat, left shaved hairs all over the bathroom sink or expected you to pick up his clothes all the time. But we sure notice all those things now! Worse still is that he probably has his own list of things he can't believe he didn't notice in you before you started living together. Maybe he did notice but he did not seem to care so much about them back then. The old saying, "Familiarity breeds contempt" can be true if we let it. All of us are human, each with our own different set of imperfections. Add to that the fact that all of us are basically selfish seems to make romance more of an impossibility rather than a hoped-for reality.

The Chase Ends

Why do some couples live so happily together for years but then as soon as they get married have countless problems in their relationship? Why can a man be so romantic until after the honeymoon, and then degenerate into an unfeeling, boring, predictable husband? ***The answer can often lie in the understanding of the security verses the insecurity of the relationship.*** A man can be so romantic when there is competition for the lady he loves. A man can sometimes move heaven and earth to win the heart of a woman but once she has been caught then the chase ends. Ironically it is romance that can win the chase for a man.

When does the chase end? The chase ends in security for the couple, when they are "tied" together in a form of commitment so the threat of anyone else winning their partner's heart is greatly reduced. The traditional word that means commitment and security and tying one's self to another is what we call marriage. Interestingly enough, when one partner becomes attracted to someone else, the offended partner can become incredibly romantic and the chase begins again. That is until the threat is removed and security settles in again. The concept of the security of a relationship can lead to taking each other for granted. "If I make the effort to be romantic or even if I don't, I will still be married to my partner tomorrow. What's the difference in the results, anyway?" Unfortunately, this attitude pushes one's relationship into a routine, predictable, unromantic tie that becomes more like an imprisoning chain. The secret is to have security without taking the other for granted, romance without predictable routine and continued chasing even though the other is already caught. The reality is in the realisation that life is too short and none of us have a guarantee on our relationship with our partner for tomorrow. We just have the here and now, which, if we make the most of, gives us memories here and now and makes tomorrow more satisfying.

The secret is to have security without taking the other for granted, romance without predictable routine and continued chasing even though the other is already caught.

Being Manly

Another reason why romance often dies is that the man never was romantic, likes being that way and seems unlikely to ever change. Many men believe real men shouldn't lower themselves to this type of behaviour that seems to them almost effeminate; others can't be bothered to make the effort, while still others believe romance is only for young (puppy) lovers and not mature, long term spouses. We will spend a lot of time on this in the next chapter.

Let me say with all of these reasons why romance dies, that I am still a great believer in marriage. The potential passion and romance it has to offer is one of life's greatest ecstasies and fulfilments. Romance of the highest kind is achievable to every couple, especially if the information and strategies outlined in this book are followed. Many couples already understand at least some of these concepts and their happiness and love lives are testimony to the fact that they have learned these secrets.

I have listed some of the main reasons why romance suffers in long term intimate relationships. Not all of them of course happen in every relationship. So don't try and see every one of these reasons being present in your own relationship. Indeed yours may have one, two or none. I have just revealed a variety of different forces I have seen at work destroying romance in a relationship often without the couple even being aware of it.

Lack of Training

With so many forces potentially working against romance and with so many marriages ending in divorce why is there so little education **before** marriage? Our society trains people for years through schooling before releasing them into the work force. We have to pass both written and practical tests for driving before we are allowed to drive a car. For so many of life's tasks we are prepared, trained and tested. But for the most important relationship in our lives what training are we given? How are we taught the intimate art of loving another imperfect human being unconditionally? Who teaches us how to **keep** the romantic fires of passion alive in our spouse?

> *How are we taught the intimate art of loving another imperfect human being unconditionally?*

How has *your* man learned? The chances are that he hasn't been prepared at all. He may have had some early role models but these could have taught him failure rather than success! It may well be that he might just be bumbling along trusting his own instincts, working at a trial and error approach to your relationship. It could very well be that your man loves you with every cell of his body but he has never been taught how to express it constantly and romantically to you, or even understands the importance and benefits of romance in his intimate relationship with you. It's not your man's fault so it's no good blaming him. So if this is true, that your man knows very little of the nature, importance, place of and the male/female differences towards romance, then what can you do to change all that? Precisely what the next chapter is all about - you are going to educate him. You're going to make sure he gets the right training that he probably has never had.

SUMMARY OF CHAPTER THREE

Why Does Romance Die?

1. It runs out of fuel or lacks the right conditions just as a candle can stop burning.
2. Newness is substituted for routine.
3. Lack of "quality time".
4. The wear and tear of idiosyncrasies.
5. The lack of incentive to capture the other's heart now that the chase has ended, and the taking of each other for granted.
6. A man's perception that romance is not manly.
7. A man's lack of training and wrong role models for the importance of romance.

4

CHAPTER FOUR

EDUCATING HIM

"The mediocre teacher tells. The good teacher explains. The superior teacher demonstrates. The great teacher inspires." (William Arthur Ward)

The first step in turning your man into a romantic is giving him the opportunity to understand the importance and nature of romance. But in order for you to do that, **you** must understand clearly the different general attitudes women and men have. So let's explore the whole concept of romance for a few pages so that you will really understand the important parts of it.

The Female View
Romance is both learned and innate in women. From early childhood the popular fairy stories are filled with princesses and Prince Charmings, with the heroes overcoming any odds to win the love of the woman and then living happily ever after. Playing with "dolls" and "dressing up" is expected play for little girls. An expression of emotion is also expected. It is okay for little girls to cry if they fall over. As girls

grow older parents consider a daughter who talks to girlfriends in her room for long periods of time quite normal. Giggling and communication with other girls about all sorts of topics is accepted and deemed appropriate.

So when a woman decides to get married she has already had a whole lifetime of expressing emotions, communicating and an orientation to romance. But women also have an innate predisposition towards romance. They are more interested in people oriented activities and experience life at a generally deeper level of communication than men. Furthermore, women are incurable romantics. Have you considered romance as being a ***need*** for a woman? Well, it is. Think of your own desires for romance and how you feel when those desires are met. Think about what lengths you would go, to be able to turn your man into the Prince Charming envied by every other woman.

Yes indeed, romance for a woman, is more than a nice extra - it is a need. This is why the romance novel industry has a ninety-nine percent female readership. It also explains why it is a multimillion-dollar business - it is meeting a need. Unfortunately this could also tell us that maybe the men in this world are not meeting that need in reality, if so much time and money is spent on romantic fantasy.

Romance for a woman, is more than a nice extra - it is a need.

Given the right conditions romance can also be an aphrodisiac. It can lower your inhibitions and heighten your sexual response, making you really crave for sexual fulfilment. Indeed romance is a high-powered tool that can have long reaching and life-changing effects. Many a woman has changed her attitude about a man who constantly uses the power of romance to woo her. The rough and tough king of Australian Rugby League, Wally Lewis, did not rely on his status and popularity in football or his physical appearance when it came to winning the woman of his dreams. When she refused his advances he did not give up but romanced her with large numbers of roses. He was not concerned with any rivals wooing her but just continued romancing her from a distance. It did the trick and they have been happily married for years. No doubt when she saw Wally through the eyes his romance had provided her, he became irresistible.

The Male View

The male childhood is filled with different toys and education. Instead of Cinderella and Snow White, boys' favourite stories are filled with action and adventure. He plays with toy soldiers, cars and things that are mechanical or "buildable". When *he* falls over he is told to be a man. How do men act? They don't show their emotions. They are strong and can't be considered "sissy". The same parents, who would think their daughter's behaviour to be normal if she talked to her friends in her room for hours, would become suspicious or worried if all their *son* ever did was talk to members of the same sex in his bedroom for hours. Generally men think in terms of logic. They make decisions supposedly not on how they feel about a matter but through a deduction on the evidence. Many men avoid crying and see it as a real sign of weakness if a man dares to cry.

This basic attitude of suppression of both positive and negative emotions is a real barrier that (dare I say it) most men carry with them into their intimate relationship. So masculinity is associated with being unemotional, self-supportive and mechanical, which leaves romance completely a female concern. Fortunately, not every man is so cold and totally unromantic but most men play this game in the company of other men. What man doesn't get a "ribbing" of sarcastic comments when he exhibits some form of romantic behaviour? For instance, if a man brought a bunch of flowers for his spouse and took them to footy practice, imagine the gibes of his unromantic mates. The whole problem is that the typical male associates romance with being effeminate, whilst he associates the antithesis of romance with masculinity.

> *So masculinity is associated with being unemotional, self-supportive and mechanical, which leaves romance completely a female concern.*

Dr James Dobson, best-selling author and psychologist puts it much better than I can state it. Below is a quotation from his book, *What Wives Wish Their Husbands Knew About Women.*

"A man can be contented with a kind of business partnership in marriage, provided sexual privileges are part of the arrangement. As long as his wife prepares his dinner each evening, is reasonably amiable, and doesn't nag him during football season, he can be satisfied. The romantic element is nice - but not necessary. However, this kind of surface relationship drives his wife utterly wild with frustration. She must have something more meaningful. Women yearn to be the special sweethearts of their men, being respected and appreciated and loved with tenderness. This is why a housewife often thinks about her husband during the day and eagerly awaits his arrival home; it explains why their anniversary is more important to her, and why he gets clobbered when he forgets it. It explains why she is constantly "reaching" for him when he is at home, trying to pull him out of the newspaper or television set; it explains why Absence of Romantic Love in My Marriage ranked so high as a source of depression among women, whereas men would have rated it somewhere in the vicinity of last place."[5]

Men could live forever without any romance but they expect that their partners should be able to do the same. They don't understand how important and how different romance is for a woman - that it is in fact, a need. Why then are so many men romantic when they are dating women in the early stages of their relationships? Primarily because many see it as a sort of means to an end. It is the done thing for men to show romantic gestures when they are chasing women but once caught men seem to think that the marriage certificate is a viable, reasonable substitute for romance. It almost seems it is viewed as a pre-courtship tradition, which is carried out for tradition's sake.

With such a completely different view of romance between the sexes how is it that intimate relationships ever survive? Well unfortunately, many of them don't and it seems the majority of those that do survive are also largely unromantic given enough time. Maybe this is why a single woman's lifestyle is so attractive to many. It offers the opportunity to be romanced by one or more men. If a woman can control the relationship to the level of commitment that she wishes, she can have the romance she desires. But there are also security and maternal needs which long for fulfilment and take away from the lustre of the single woman's lifestyle. Can you have it both ways? Can you have security, a cherished home (even children) and still live with a romantic Prince Charming? The answer is definitely "Yes", no matter how unromantic your partner's attitude seems at the moment.

A lot of men show they are romantics when they are dating women and if they have done this in the past then it proves that they are capable of it in the future. The drive in a man to win the heart of the woman he loves can be extremely strong. Think of the effort many men go to if their lady "plays hard to get", or breaks off a relationship with them. This may have happened in your own relationship's history. It just demonstrates that men deep down know that romance does increase their chances of winning their women's hearts. Is it not so much like hu**man** behaviour that we don't change until we have to - until the pressure is put on? But that is never the best way to change.

> *A lot of men show they are romantics when they are dating women and if they have done this in the past then it proves that they are capable of it in the future.*

You could threaten to leave your partner unless he becomes romantic but it will not work. It may appear to work, at least for a while but external pressure or threats do not bring about the best change. Conversely the most effective and lasting change is brought about when a man changes for his own reasons, to fulfil his own needs, to change for his own approval not because someone else wants him to. In fact many of us do the opposite to what others want us to do, if for no other reason than to prove we alone have the power of our own autonomy.

So how does a man change for his own reasons? How does a man break free from this typical attitude that men are supposed to be unemotional, unromantic and "he-mannish"? The first step is for a man to grasp the idea that romance is another aspect of his masculinity.

1. Romance Is Masculine

Probably the most popularised lover in history was Casanova. His name has since become synonymous for a man popular with the ladies. Regardless of what we think about him today, Casanova had a few desirable talents. Firstly, he was talented enough to play the violin for paid work when he was a youth. But he was also a poet and knew how to make an entertaining and witty conversation. He seemed to ooze with charm and attracted people everywhere. He mixed it with the best in society. He had contacts of the wealthiest and most famous people in Europe and was seen by many as having power transcending geographical and political boundaries. Add these attributes together and you can easily see how he was such a success at alluring women. But Casanova was also a romantic. Add romance to these other characteristics (take away any sleaziness) and we don't have a man wanting to seduce women, we have a line of women wanting to be seduced by this type of man!

Many women may desire these good Casanova characteristics in men, but what do men think about them? Men probably have mixed feelings towards Casanova. Some think he was a very effeminate, lady's man. Others may give him the benefit of the doubt seeing they never met him personally. But one common thought among men stands out. Casanova, however he did it, was a "woman-conqueror". He knew how to use this power because women flocked to him as if they were under his spell. Many men are almost jealous of him for it, in other words they wish they had the same power over women, the same success with women that Casanova appears to have had.

The whole point is this; **although the romantic image of Casanova may appeal to a woman, what appeals to a man is that Casanova was a woman-seducer, a woman conqueror.** It also explains the attitude men have of other men who are highly successful with women. This is how it goes. If a man has sex with a high number of women then he is given the grand and lofty title of "stud". He is often envied by his peers because they think he is the ultimate of masculinity. His mates will look him over in the change room for any **physical** sign that gives away his secret with women. They may do on-the-spot, quick comparisons with themselves, checking biceps and chest size and any other "body proportions". But no physical evidence is the secret to the long term, successful Casanova. Indeed if you have seen the portrait of Casanova you probably, as any woman would, be turned off straight away at his big nose and un-handsomely face. But also true has been many women's disappointment when they take the physical, "masculine" stud to bed or try and make a lifelong partner out of him.

So why do men hold in awe with jealousy the local stud? Why do they wish that they could be a woman-conqueror and be seen as so very masculine? The answer is the male ego. In the world of the male ego the young male quickly realises there is fierce competition. Every man's male ego encourages him to be successful with women. But just as we said earlier that men's minds were oriented to physical thought patterns, so the male ego is oriented to believing that **physical** success with women is the key to real masculinity.

> *The male ego is oriented to believing that physical success with women is the key to real masculinity.*

This also explains why the majority of people who go to relationship counsellors are women. So many men are reluctant to have **outside** help with their intimate relationship problems. It is less threatening for a male to say a problem doesn't exist in his relationship than to admit to his male ego that he may have failed in his "success" with a woman. There is one exception, however. Whenever there is a physical problem in marriage, especially "on the woman's side" (for example, low sexual desire in the woman, which is really a joint problem but often seen by men as an exclusively female-caused problem), then the pressure is put on **her** to get **herself** sorted out.

This also explains why many men's fantasies include the concept of a man being in control of a woman to the extreme. Such an idea is often portrayed in the porn industry where women are portrayed almost as slaves who desperately crave the slightest attention from the male stud (symbolic of the male viewer). As Warren Farrell puts it in his book, *Why Men Are The Way They Are*, "Pornography appeals to men's primary fantasy - Access to as many beautiful women without the risk of rejection."[6]

The male ego is quite fragile and very susceptible to rejection. I know of some men who have constantly gone out with women and then after a few months have broken the relationship off and the male seems as if he has suffered little or no loss. But then when someone has got in first and broken the relationship off with the man - then that has completely the opposite effect. Then the male is rejected and he hardly ever seems able to get over the breakup. The people that play these games think there is a reward for their ego, when really it is just preserving an insecure one. Unfortunately there are too many Hollywood films, pornography, and glossy magazines that feed to men (and women) the idea that physical success with women *alone* is the ultimate goal for the male ego because true masculinity is physical success.

Right now you're probably saying that you think it's a big job to retrain your partner's ego and that you have to be some kind of psychologist to do that. Well, don't be disappointed because that's not what's expected of you. On the contrary you only have to get him to understand what a woman's (specifically your) definition of masculinity is. How do you do that? By understanding that *romance must be linked to his ego. The man himself must see being romantic as an increase to his ego.*

As I have just explained, the trouble with most men is that they see romance as a *decrease* to their ego and masculinity. They see flowers and romance as too soft, sissy, and only for a womaniser and the effeminate. The underlying thought is "I'm too macho and masculine for that. I should be able to command my lady's love by physical advantages, if not, then something must be missing in my masculine manhood (insecure ego)."

What you are going to learn to do is to turn this whole concept around so that *he sees it as a macho thing to be a romantic.* This is not as hard as you may at first think because who is it that builds the ego in your man? It's not, fortunately, your partner's male companions. It's not even the man himself. It has been and always will be the women in his life. Firstly it was his mother but now and primarily, it is you and it will be you for a long time. This fragile male ego in your man is in your hands to either destroy through criticism or build and shape through your approval and appreciation.

> *He has to see it as a macho thing to be a romantic.*

So far we have looked at only one point in what area you can reveal a different perspective to your man. We have spent quite a few pages exploring the masculine view men have and we have also looked at the male ego. This is so that you can understand what you are up against, how he is thinking and why this area is so important. In order for you to influence someone else you have to have it clear in your own mind, otherwise you will lead others around in circles and you will not be able to share with them what you have learned. We are now going to look at some other areas that you will have to address in bringing this information to your man. Then after we have it clear what we are going to reveal to him, we will turn to the ***how*** of imparting this knowledge to him.

2. Romance Is Power Because It Is The Strongest Female Aphrodisiac.

Once a man understands that he can be romantic and still be perceived as very masculine (or in his woman's eyes more masculine than ever) he can then start to appreciate the feelings that he can generate in a woman. True romance from the man she loves is the greatest aphrodisiac for a woman. Alcohol is often used as an aphrodisiac to try and increase a woman's sexual desire. But alcohol only lowers a person's inhibitions and therefore isn't a true aphrodisiac. Romance does both and when used in the right circumstances it is a strong, powerful tool to increase a woman's sexual arousal.

Romance does have power but how many men consciously understand this power and how many go out of their way to use romance in long term relationships when a woman is feeling sexually low? Unfortunately, I know of many men who take completely the wrong approach when their partners don't show the same enthusiasm that the men wished their spouses would have. Usually the man will blame his partner for the problem, whereas if he just understood the power of romance he would know that with a little romantic effort on his part he could completely change his partner's whole attitude to sex, from duty to delight, to even desire. We will explore this concept in detail in chapter seven.

It's funny how the word aphrodisiac gets people's attention so quickly. Everyone becomes intensely interested in the subject once they hear it. Men especially though, because of the fact that it is seen as "power" over the fairer sex. And every male is immediately interested in something which in his hands makes him desirable to women. Isn't it strange how man has searched for thousands of years to find a true aphrodisiac when romance has always been there begging to do its job? Isn't it also strange that man is still looking for aphrodisiacs in **physical** form? Still thinking in the physical sense, man still tries mixing various potions hoping to chance upon a mystical love potion.

> *Isn't it strange how man has searched for thousands of years to find a true aphrodisiac when romance has always been there begging to do its job?*

I have at times, when speaking to groups, demonstrated it this way. I have held in my hand a dark coloured bottle. Then I have claimed, that in this bottle was the formulae for the most powerful female aphrodisiac known to mankind. The potion's components were easily accessible to all, and it could be reconstructed time and time again. How much would some men be willing to pay for such a foolproof aphrodisiac? Imagine what great advantages it would give to a man that owned it. Some men would do just about anything to get it I'm sure. What is in the bottle? Just a piece of paper with the word **"romance"** written on it. Yet romance does live up to all these claims as the most powerful female aphrodisiac. Nothing else comes close and yet so many men don't understand this secret.

When a man understands the true power of romance, and can be trusted to use it properly and not abuse it, it is not only a power that excites his masculinity but it can also be very fulfilling to him. Take for instance the man who has been complaining for years of his partner's sexual lethargy until he finally stops blaming her and starts to use romance to express his love for her. He learns to express his love for his partner, to spend quality time with her, to communicate his feelings to her and learns the proper way to encourage those responses he has maybe only ever before fantasised. He commits to connecting with her at a very deep level. Now he can feel satisfied in himself that he knows which are the right buttons to push to fulfil a need in his partner so that she feels satisfied to give the responses she has wanted to give for a long time but has not been able to give. Yes, romance is power but it is also very fulfilling and satisfying for a man to use that power so that both partners can enjoy throughout their whole lifetime, the passion that newly-weds have.

3. Romance is a physical benefit to him.

Remember how I said before that romance was a need for a woman? What is the corresponding need in intimate relationships for a man? Well, maybe we can find the answer by turning to the publishing industry. Romance novels comprise forty percent of all paperback book sales. Yes, certainly romance is a need for a woman. But when we look to find the biggest selling magazines which men buy we find they were traditionally *Playboy* and *Penthouse*.

Men don't see romance as a turn-on but they do have a built-in, fascination with physical, naked, female bodies. You see men are turned on by the physical dimensions in a relationship. It's just male DNA. That Y chromosome has a lot to answer for. A man's head turns to give him a second look when he sees female flesh being revealed even if it is only slight or subtle. So fulfilment of their physical need, to both see their female partner naked and to have sex with her is a high priority for a man's intimate relationship. In fact many men relate the health of their intimate relationship to how well their sex life is (women however, often regard the closeness of their relationship as the sign of whether their sex life is good or not).

> *Men don't see romance as a turn-on but they do have a built-in, fascination with physical, naked, female bodies.*

This fascination men have with female bodies is now everywhere in society. Since the introduction of the internet into everyone's lives, women's bodies are plastered everywhere to cater to this masculine fixation. It is no secret that porn has made billions of dollars since the start of the internet. But it has also evolved now into making Instagram sensations and internet influencers out of any young woman who is prepared to snap any number of pics in either a bikini or body hugging, revealing sportswear. Is it any wonder that Kylie Jenner at the age of only 21 was the youngest ever self made billionaire, thanks mainly to her huge social media followers?

So what has this physical orientation that a man has towards women to do with romance? Well, once a man understands that romance is an aphrodisiac to his partner and that it will lower her inhibitions and create more desire in her for him, then he starts to experience benefits to his own physically oriented needs. If a woman has increased desire for her man because of romance, then it's only natural to assume that **both** partners will enjoy the physical climax. Romance leads to heightened physical responses. Romance prepares a woman for lovemaking both physically and mentally, by creating desire to experience the physical expression of love.

> *Romance leads to heightened physical responses.*

Let me demonstrate it this way. Many men wish to have sex with their partners but they are totally void of romance, and neither do they prepare their wives for lovemaking. So even though the woman might be tired and view sex at this time as an interruption and a disturbance, the man will still try and "physically" stimulate her, to make sure she is aware of his sexual intentions. So if he is lucky, even if out of a sense of duty, the woman allows him to use her body even though she knows she will receive no pleasure, just inconvenience. This one-way sex unfortunately happens far too often. Indeed for many relationships this is the majority of sex and for some the only form of sex. My view of this type of relationship is that it is only one small step away from necrophilia - making love to a corpse! You see necrophilia isn't popular or wanted by men - it is only desired by the abnormal and perverted and possibly those who can't make it with real, live people in the real world.

Men want just the opposite. Their male ego cries out for their masculinity to be craved for and desired. Men are turned on by a woman who is sexually alive and is interested in fulfilling their physical needs as if it were her need too. So when the woman becomes sexually alive because romance has created desire for lovemaking in her, the man can begin to enjoy the physical side of the relationship ten times more. Given the choice, a man will choose hot, passionate, romantic, two-way lovemaking every time in preference to one way, dead sex.

4. Romance Substitutes Zest For Routine

Once a man experiences the aphrodisiac effect upon his partner, and how the physical side of their relationship is improved, he starts to see the potential romance has for his relationship with his mate. Remember how I said that men tend to measure their relationship by how good their sex life is and so as romance increases the quality of their sex life, a man feels positive about the rest of his relationship (and his life in general). His needs are being met and so he is in a better position to consider the **other** needs of his partner. This can be a sort of chain reaction effect upon the other areas of the relationship. Furthermore, both can experience a general zest for life when routine has been conquered by romance. When a couple are in love and are expressing it freely to each other they become more positive in every area of their lives.

"In 1985 the American magazine *Psychology Today* reported a study where two-hundred and forty university students were asked to look at photographs of strangers. The study found that people who were in love consistently found the strangers more attractive than those who weren't in love - but only when they were questioned beforehand about their love life. The psychologist running the study theorised that discussing their love life may have aroused the students, giving them positive feelings to the world at large". (As quoted in Cleo magazine, June 1990 p111.)

So romance can even be better for both you and your partner's health and your general attitude to life. Often both men and women feel trapped in routine. Romance provides that change, that zest, that spontaneity that we all enjoy so much. To think that romance is the key to so much - if only men knew!

To think that romance is the key to so much - if only men knew!

5. Romance Is Fun And Not That Difficult

When the adrenaline blast of romance injects that life-giving zest into a relationship and the lives of those connected with it, both partners realise that it can be fun and exhilarating. Everybody likes to be around fun people. Fun and happiness have a magnetism that draw us all. When a man experiences the fun of romance and the happy spark it generates, he finds it is more pleasant to keep it alive than to lose it (it is also easier to keep alive than to resurrect it or find it if it has died).

So not only does romance become fun but also the male partner realises that it isn't as difficult to keep alive as he first pictured.

For some reason men have this myth about romance requiring tons of effort and drive, heaps of money and half their life in time. But once a **commitment** and a proper attitude towards romance are established, the cost and effort is very small, especially compared to the benefits for both sides in the relationship.

6. Romance is a Woman's Need and a Man's Responsibility

This concept may not be appreciated by every man but it will hit home on some. The man it will work on will be the man who has a high sense of duty to his spouse. He is the one who has the traditional concept that a man is the breadwinner who provides the financial security of the relationship. Many men who have this concept, believe their responsibility ends there, that this traditional, masculine role relieves them of any further emotional or domestic duties and affords them the privileges of a faithful and adoring woman. This male type may be a little overstated but depending upon how much of this attitude is present is how effective this approach could be - if he sees romance as an extension of his "husbandly" responsibilities.

In order for a man to accept that romance is his responsibility, he must understand that romance is indeed a need for his spouse. He must understand that it isn't just a trivial need but a major need that deserves to be fulfilled just as his needs do. Some men have a very high sense of duty, of meeting their responsibilities. However the key is that they must understand that romance is a real, **constant** need for a woman and not just a fleeting desire now and again. The man has to realise that an ongoing need deserves **ongoing** commitment to fulfil it.

> *The man has to realise that an ongoing need deserves ongoing commitment to fulfil it.*

7. He Has To See Your Desire For Him To Be Romantic And The Happiness It Will Bring.

Rather, or in addition to your mate seeing romance as his responsibility, your man must see your intense desire for him to be a romantic partner. It is one thing for a man to understand intellectually that women have a built in need for romance. It is another thing for a man to see that need personalised in the form of desire and hope in his own spouse and to see the potential happiness it will bring. We all like to please others and like to receive the due recognition, appreciation and positive, warm inside feeling of doing something good for another person. I guess it can be likened to the positive feelings you experience when giving a gift to someone else (especially a child). Unless we are so totally self-absorbed, narcissistic and unwilling to help anyone else, there is a special happiness received when we create happiness for others, especially for those we love the most. So let him see the desire you have for romance and how happy and satisfied you will be when he meets those desires.

8. Romance Must Be Initiated By The Man.

This concept has to be reinforced so that your man clearly understands this important point. Part of the nature of romance is that it often has a sense of mystery or surprise for the woman. A woman gets more of a thrill and excitement when she is given a romantic gift or is invited out on a romantic date straight away rather than being told she is going to be given a bunch of flowers on the twenty-fifth of next month. If she has a lot of time to consider the *possibility* of the gift rather than the gift itself she may be tempted to remind him or wonder if he will remember (this especially happens if no more is mentioned about it by the man). The woman has all that time to think of the negative side (what if…) instead of being caught up in the beauty of it all. So although a romantic gift can be planned behind the scenes, it is best for the receiver not to be aware of it until it is presented.

The man has to understand that romance falls completely flat if he has to be reminded, prompted, prodded, given clues, doesn't lead in romance or doesn't care for all the details of romance himself. Furthermore a man has to understand that in order to receive the full effect of romance he has to take the initiative. Romance just isn't romance to a woman if she is always the one who suggests romance or is the only one who is romantic. Women have the need for romance that only a man can fulfil. A woman can't be expected to fulfil that need herself. If he does take the initiative he shows he wants to be romantic, that he has the right attitude towards romance, and that she is worth him making her the centre of his romantic intentions. By taking the initiative it communicates a desire to express the special love a man has for a woman.

Romance just isn't romance to a woman if she is always the one who suggests romance or is the only one who is romantic.

A man also has to understand that there is a right way and a wrong way to be romantic. For instance, a bunch of flowers maybe a romantic gift but they have to be given romantically. The man has to show that he wants to give this romantic gift and that his attitude matches the gift. In order for a gift to be truly romantic, the man must have the right attitude - he can't portray the "now I have fulfilled my obligation so I hope you're happy" approach. Even if he jokes sarcastically about it, plays down its magic or doesn't give the gift romantically, he can lose so much of the shine of the romantic gesture. Yes, there is much more to romance than just an act, it must:

- be initiated by the male
- have an element of surprise or mystery
- have a **genuine** attitude accompanying it.

9. Romance Sends The Signal That The Man Is Prioritising The Relationship

What a man often fails to recognise is the implication of romantic acts. For him to go out of his way and take the effort for a romantic gesture, means far more than the act itself. It is not limited to the fact that he thought it would bring pleasure to his partner. The main message it sends to his woman is that he is prioritising the relationship. Think about it. It is nice to receive a bunch of flowers, but the gesture has a deeper meaning. The fact that he has made the effort to think about getting them, then to go out of his way to get them and then give them to you is nice. But the fact that he knows to do it, the fact that he knows the gesture will bring pleasure to you and the fact that he actually did it, that has the greater meaning. Back in the first chapter we talked about what a man can bring to the relationship. The third point is his strength. It is not that a woman needs a strong man to move the furniture around the house every weekend. What she needs is a man strong enough to take the lead in their relationship so that she doesn't have to constantly worry about the health of their relationship. Romance does exactly that. It shows a strong man who is willing to take the lead in fulfilling his woman's needs but also that he is willingly, off his own back, taking the lead in putting his relationship way up in his list of priorities. This man instantly eases his woman's concerns about any insecurities she might have about the relationship. She is instantly reassured through action rather than any defensive words a man might mouth in response to insecurities a woman might attempt to express. Romance helps to remove a lot of the insecurities a woman might have in regards to the relationship. This is another important reason as to why it is so important for a woman in a long term relationship. We will return to this concept in the final chapter to understand how insecurities concerning the relationship inhibit connection, romance and even sexuality. When insecurities are dealt with, a woman can relax. When a woman relaxes, she doesn't over-invest in negative aspects of the relationship. She then has more energy to devote to connecting and inviting her man to be closer to her instead of allowing her anxieties to build defensive barriers to her inviting her man to be closer to her. Remember what romance signals.

These nine areas are all important, however some may be more important than others when it comes to *your* man. We have surveyed the principles and generalisations but there will always be individual exceptions. That may be the hard part for you but in going over these nine areas with your man, in order to educate him, it is not the information that will cause any objections from him. Even if he doesn't agree with or catch onto one area it will not hurt him to be presented with it. It is true, however, many men may see the areas more clearly in other men rather than themselves.

The objections will be more from *how* the information is presented to them. If they take it personally, if it is presented negatively, if they are asked to change or else, or if they are told or shown to be doing it wrong all these years, you will find more barriers than ever towards them being romantic. So let's turn now to the important art of *how* to educate your man in the areas we have just looked at.

SUMMARY OF CHAPTER FOUR

Romance is a need for a woman.
    Romance can be seen as unmanly by a man.
    Men can use romance as a means to an end but will often stop romance when the end is achieved.
    Men show they can be romantic during courtship.

A man must want to be a romantic for his own reasons, which may include:

1. The belief that romance is masculine. He must see romance as an increase to his ego and a power of attraction to a woman.
2. Romance is power because it is the strongest female aphrodisiac. It is satisfying for a man to be able to push all the right buttons and really turn his partner on.
3. A man's physical needs are more likely to be met in response to the more romantic he is. Romance heightens physical desires in women.
4. Romance provides zest and happiness. It takes the boredom out of routine.
5. Romance is easy and is lots of fun.
6. Romance is a real need for his partner and it is his responsibility to fulfil it because a woman can't fulfil it for herself.
7. A man needs to understand his partner's desire for him to lead in romance and the satisfaction and happiness it will bring to both.

Romance must be initiated and led by the man.
He must lead in romance and care for the details of dates.
He must include an element of surprise or mystery.
He must have a genuinely positive attitude towards romance.

Romance sends the signal that the man is prioritising the relationship

5

CHAPTER FIVE

THE ART OF HOW TO EDUCATE HIM

"Men's emotions are like an invisible clitoris – you should not be too direct too quickly!" - Patricia Love & Steven Stosny

Communication analysis

The very first task is to assess how well you and your mate communicate to each other. Are those communication avenues open in your relationship at the present time? Does he genuinely listen to what you say and does he usually understand the message you try to get across to him? Does he take the time and the interest to make sure that what you say is the message he has received and understands? Are there any communication blocks or barriers in your relationship at the present? Does he have a habit of reacting the opposite way to how you wish in order to get even for some past offence? The answers to these questions will determine whether you can talk directly to him without the fear of obstacles in your communication or without him reacting the wrong way. If you are confident that you and your man have good communication then you are ready to educate him once you have the information firm in your own mind. If, on the other hand, you have poor communication with your man or you know of some barrier between you, then you will have to fix it so you can communicate well before you even begin to take the first step. It is really beyond the scope of this book to build or rebuild better communication bridges. You can buy some excellent books on this topic or you can search online and find some excellent resources on communication in intimate relationships. The important point is that you make sure your communication with your spouse is the best it can be when you approach him with some new information.

Sometimes we can take completely the wrong communication approach when we are trying to get our message across to someone. For instance, if we are paid a compliment how often do we play it down or even disagree with the person, quietly hoping inside that they will persist or add to their compliment? This is the wrong approach to reinforcing this behaviour. It does work spasmodically and might show humility, but it is not as effective as thanking the person.

Sometimes we get so used to playing things down we are afraid that if we say we like a thing it might stop. So we will keep playing it down, maybe even making a joke out of it, telling them how silly they may be, so that hopefully they will continue to seek our illusive approval. If you are guilty of this, as many are, then you must get out of the habit and communicate openly without playing games and learn to reinforce by approval. It's time to leave our insecurities behind and be positive, direct, approachable and clearly understandable. Positive people attract other people. We all would rather associate with positive people we understand and know exactly where we stand with them. Make sure that you don't send mixed signals, as that only frustrates your man. Sending mixed signals may make us think it adds mystery or excitement but it doesn't. It only adds frustration and confusion to the other person receiving the communication. Leave the mystery and excitement to romance, learn and practise clear, sound communication and you are well on the way to educating your man without confusion.

The Invitation

What I suggest, once you are sure your communication is what it should be, is that you make a special date with your spouse. What you are going to do on this date is talk over with him the points about romance outlined in the last chapter.

Firstly, you must pick the time carefully. You may find the best time is a day when he is not working, so he will be fresh and relaxed rather than uptight or tired from a hard day's work. Make it as early as possible if it's in the evening, so that he can't grow tired before the end of the date.

Secondly, you must choose the place carefully. Don't fall into the trap of just telling him about romance at your home. You must get away somewhere new. This is where you will introduce change straight away by going away together somewhere new from your usual environment. Try and choose somewhere romantic, like a nice restaurant where you can have a delicious dinner. If you go out together you have removed the possibility of distractions such as the home phone ringing, visitors calling, television programs, different amusements or jobs competing for his attention. You also need the time commitment from him so that you have the opportunity to say all that you want to say.

Thirdly, when you invite your man out on this date advertise it as something really worthwhile for both of you. You might even want to build some suspense and curiosity in him by telling him you have some exciting ideas to talk to him about, but how he has to wait until the date. The main point is that you present it in very positive, glowing terms. Tell him how you think **he** is going to be interested in what you have to share with him, and how you can see very exciting benefits to him. Make sure you advertise it in general terms but that the positive benefits to him are real without elaborating any further. Furthermore, gently remind him so that he can't forget the date or fill that time with some other activity unintentionally. Make sure also that you don't allow too long a gap between the invitation and the date. Give him enough time to plan and be curious but not so long that he will become suspicious or worried. Several days to a week at the most will be fine.

The Date Itself

Don't go on the date to talk about romance until you have read this book in its entirety. There is a lot of information in it and ideas and concepts later in the book will teach you how to build intimacy and how to raise intimacy tolerance in your man and yourself. It will also explain to you how not to get your man offside by activating his defence mechanisms. So once you have finished then you can come back and plan how you will run your introduction to romance 101. The best way will be to start with a series of questions. The world's best teachers always taught through the use of pertinent questioning to invoke a thoughtful response without debating. Here are a series of questions you can use to encourage your man to think about romance.

Questions For Her To Ask Him

1. When did you realise you wanted to be with me forever?
2. What are some of the things we used to do that you miss now?
3. What would you like more of in our relationship?
4. If you wanted to impress me and money was no object, what would be the most romantic thing you would do for me?
5. What do you like about me the most?
6. What new sex position would you like to try?
7. Describe your perfect valentine's day.
8. When do you feel I love you the most?
9. What is the one thing you could do to bring yourself closer to me?
10. What is the best way to get your attention?
11. What ideas could you come up with to be more romantic?

Questions For Him To Ask Her

1. When did you realise you wanted to be with me forever?

2. What are some of the things we used to do that you miss now?
3. What would you like more of in our relationship?
4. How important is romance to you in your relationship?
5. What makes you feel close to your partner?
6. What do you like about me the most?
7. What new sex position would you like to try?
8. Describe your perfect valentine's day.
9. When do you feel I love you the most?
10. How do you see our love years from now?
11. When do I most look manly and irresistible in your eyes?

These questions are an opportunity to talk positively about your relationship. They are not an exercise with the goal of criticising your mate. They are an opportunity to say what turns you on and what you want more of in the relationship. You could ask one question each so that your man doesn't feel it's an interrogation. You do have an advantage because you will have seen the questions before and can take your time on how romance will play an important role in your answers. You may very well be pleasantly surprised about your man's answers. He may give you some deep and very meaningful responses. But consider how often we do something like this in everyday life. Sometimes we just need the quietness to sit and reflect on these really important questions. They are important because they open the door to us communicating and getting what matters most to us. Plus they also help to build intimacy.

However you answer your questions, it is important that you start positively and that he can see the benefits to himself. Don't make it like a school lesson. Don't in any way make it negative by intimating that he has being doing things wrong by not being a romantic. Don't start with what the wrong view of masculinity is but refer to his romantic deeds in the past and how they have turned you on. You have to encourage the things you want repeated, so make sure you bring up all the romantic deeds he has done and how you appreciate this side of him. Assume that romance is a part of him, and he will assume it too. Keep it positive and you can expect a positive response.

> **Make sure you bring up all the romantic deeds he has done and how you appreciate this side of him.**

By keeping a positive approach and complementing his romantic side and his romantic gestures in the past, you will prevent him from being defensive. Appreciate him rather than criticise and use "I" words rather than "you" words. For example, concentrate on your own positive feelings of what it does for *you* when he has shown his romantic side in the past. Try and present the ideas in an enthusiastic way so that he will catch the enthusiasm with you. Make sure you don't ask for a commitment from him too early in the conversation but include him by getting him to respond with his ideas and thoughts.

One of the oldest techniques used by salesmen is getting the customer to choose between two alternative choices, either of which are satisfactory for the salesman. For example, a salesman may ask "If you were to buy this product how would you be likely to pay for it? By cash or monthly instalments?" Either answer gets the consumer's mind off the commitment to purchase the product and just gets the customer thinking along the lines of assuming he or she will buy it by thinking of how he or she will pay for it.

This principle can also be used when you sell the idea of romance to your man. By asking him how his creative mind could think of new ideas for romantic times in your relationship, by getting him to relate his definition of romance and what his idea of the most romantic encounter would be if money were no problem - you get him to assume himself being romantic (or buying the product of romance you are trying to sell him). By getting him to visualise himself in this romantic role and by him understanding and imagining the benefits for himself, you are selling the idea to him so that he will **want** the product of romance.

When buying anything the consumer must always see the benefits the product has for himself.

> **When buying anything the consumer must always see the benefits the product has for himself.**

Furthermore, if he disagrees with you from the beginning, **don't disagree with him** and turn the evening into a verbal war. That is not the point of this date. Remember the point is to let him see what benefits there are for both of you in him being romantic, once he is educated about romance and sees how important it is in his own relationship with you. By not disagreeing with him you show an attitude of an open mind, which is the attitude you want him to have. Just say, "maybe so" or something similar but keep pressing on with what you want him to understand. Even if he has the wrong impression at the start, if you have the right attitude and keep explaining to him about romance he will start to see that it isn't a threat to him but something beneficial to him as well as to you and your relationship.

Another tried and tested salesman's pitch is to get the person to list any barriers that would stop them from purchasing the product. You can use this principle by asking your man if there would be anything that would stop him from being *more* of a romantic spouse. If he lists some reasons then you can deal with them once they are out in the open where you are aware of them. Ask how you can overcome them together. Get him on your side and ask what he suggests to overcome those reasons that may hamper him being romantic. In this way they become a common enemy rather than excuses on his behalf. Furthermore, once he has listed the reasons that may hold him back from being a romantic, he will realise that once those barriers are dealt with he has no reason to be unromantic. In other words, he has in fact committed himself in a default way, to being a romantic.

Ask him also if he has any questions or fears of things that would stop him and resolve them tonight! Don't be afraid of questions, as they are part of the learning process, helping him get the information right in his own mind. Tell him you appreciate how well he has listened and how you know he will give it a fair go. Tell him how turned on and excited you are already just talking about his romantic side and the happiness and thrill it gives you. Paint a picture of how happy the two of you will be and how other couples will be envious of you. Explain to him how other women will wish their men could be romantic like him. Sell the product of romance. Make him eager to try it. It will be the best purchase he has ever made!

Suppose after everything he still objects to the idea. What are you going to do? What you must do is get a commitment from him even if it is only a small one. Try to get him to commit himself to romance indefinitely but if he won't do this then try for a shorter period. For instance, if he objects to the idea, try to get him to commit himself to being a romantic for one month. If you can get him to commit himself to a trial period then that is a great start. If he still doesn't accept the trial period maybe you can persuade him to make a bet with you that your relationship will be so much happier and better for both of you if he tries it for one month. If he doesn't accept the bet he will be admitting that you would be right and he doesn't want his relationship with you to be happy. You will have to assess his reasons very carefully why he doesn't want his relationship to be the best it can be. Fortunately these men are in the minority. Don't come down too quickly. Aim high and expect high. The trial period and bet ideas are more of a last resort than the best approach to use. So make sure you try everything else first.

> *What you must do is get a commitment from him even if it is only a small one.*

The positive side is that many men aren't romantic because they never realised how important it is and so all they need is to have it explained to them and reminded now and again. To many men this will be all it takes. When they see how much it will make you happy then out of their love for you they will want to please you. Then when they understand the benefits to themselves they will have an added incentive.

Some men are not romantic because they have never directly and seriously been asked before. He might have been asked before but laughed it away (because he felt threatened by an insecure male ego), or he might have sarcastically cut the idea to bits (because of his idea of romance being effeminate or anti-masculine, or because of the presence of others or the thought of another's reaction to romance). But now alone, quietly and seriously with you on this evening date he has to consider it. That may be all it takes.

Now he is cornered seriously, give him a door he can take to get out of his corner. Let this door be a door he can choose to take so that he can convince himself that this is the way **he** wishes to go - that it is in his best interests to be a romantic. In this way he makes the decision without coercion, which will be a far more lasting decision than if you try and make it for him. Some men may just have slowly and insidiously allowed romance in their relationship to slide away. It doesn't take a conscious act as if a man gets up one morning and says, "I'm not going to be romantic any more". It is usually just replaced by routine and time pressures as priorities get out of order.

Presenting The Ideas Of This Book

You may not be able to present all of the ideas in this whole book to your man on this initial night. In fact, not all of them may be appropriate to your man anyway. Be careful not to overwhelm him with lots of information but just get across the major points. Explain to him **in your own words** your view of romance but how it is a need for **all** women. There may be other ideas that you think are more important to share with him which are found later in the book which is another reason why you need to read the whole of the book first. The main object is for you to practise connection and for your man to realise the influence romance has on the two of you for the better.

Think about how you are going to present romance to him as being an increase to his ego. Give him the vision of how you see him - and how he will see himself - as being very masculine, very sexy, very confident, very romantic, and very happy. Get him to understand that your view of him will not be unique to you but all women will perceive him in this light because of every woman's need and orientation to romance. It is very important that you present these ideas in a very positive framework. Make sure you use lots of examples from his past to convince him that he is romantic deep down. Convince him that he does have the potential to be the most romantic guy on earth. Give him a romantic name to live up to and encourage him to repeat his romantic gestures by appreciating them.

Look for what seems to provide him with the best incentives to be a romantic. It may be the thought of it being an aphrodisiac to you. It may be the closeness you both will feel in your relationship. It may be the physical, sexual rewards he can see for himself. Whatever it is, (there are different reasons which appeal to different men) make sure you notice the ones that appeal to him and explore their potential. Draw him out and get him to respond to each point you present to him so you can gauge what areas appeal to him the most. Emphasise the ones you get the most positive reaction from and leave the ones, if there are any, he may have a negative reaction to.

You will increase his male ego if you view him as a romantic and how this increases your view of him, as a man. In other words, give the romantic side of him approval that it is very manly. Build his confidence that he is most manly when he is at his most romantic. This will have the result that in order for him to increase his male ego (see his male ego as high) he will be convinced that he has to be more romantic. By verbalising to him what makes him more desirable to you - him being romantic - you are educating him into understanding what he can do practically and specifically to build his own self confidence and male ego.

When you present the concepts of this book of how romance is a need to a woman and also how the male needs to be the initiator or leader in romance, a way of making it real to him is to liken it to his own sexual needs in the relationship. For example, you might liken a woman in a relationship going without romance to a man going without sexual relations. How would a man like to practise abstinence in his relationship, or how long would he go before complaining? Make sure you put it in the third person by stating it as a man and his partner, rather than yourself and himself. By putting it in the third person as I have done, it doesn't put blame on your man because you are speaking hypothetically - using some other non-specific person to make your point. In this way your man will see the point without becoming defensive. In relation to the area on initiation it can be likened to how a man would take to having to remind his partner all the time for sex in the relationship. How long would a man be happy with only himself wanting, initiating or asking for sex? By showing how "romance is to a woman what sex is to a man", a man can understand that it is not a trivial issue but one that demands his full attention.

> *By showing how "romance is to a woman what sex is to a man", a man can understand that it is not a trivial issue but one that demands his full attention.*

Hopefully the ideas presented so far will be enough to convince your man that he will want to be romantic and that he must be romantic at any cost. Probably the problem for ninety-five percent of men will not be getting convinced about the necessity of romance on this date. Rather, for many men it will be to continue to keep the initiative in romance and keep romance fresh and new, rather than predictable. If at all possible you want to keep your man on side and look at the idea of romance together as a couple, rather than having two sides of pro and anti-romance.

After The Date

Spending time together connecting and intentionally making your relationship the focus of the time spent together should ensure the night would have been a very romantic time in itself. Especially if you have spent some of the time during the date brainstorming creative ways of being romantic together. You may not have been out for a meal together like this for a while, and so now is the time for you to show what you have been saying, to be true. That romance is pleasurable, and fun for both of you, and leads to greater intimacy.

This is another reason why you are to make sure the date goes smoothly and to get your man on your side by helping him to think of new ways to create romance in your relationship. The idea is that as soon as you win your man over to the idea of romance and get a commitment from him, then don't go on labouring the point. You can still talk about romantic ideas but remember once he is with you, you don't need to convince him as if he hasn't been convinced. Say what you want to say to him, make sure he understands the reasons for romance, get a commitment from him and then make the rest of the evening a romantic rather than a conversational date. Give him the chance to talk about things he wants to talk about. Talk about other things that may not be directly and overtly points about romance, but may still be of a romantic nature that may continue to make this date romantic. Things like pleasant memories, future holidays, hopes and dreams, hobbies and enjoyable activities.

By making at least the later part of the date specifically romantic you are getting your man to realise that he does enjoy romance, that it is fun and easily accomplished and enjoyed. You are also setting the scene for him to experience the benefits of romance for himself.

Follow Up

Finally, even before the date closes or sometime very soon after, you should arrange a follow up date or time when you can reflect on romance again. This is very important for a few reasons. Firstly, because it gives the man an incentive to get his romantic self-organised before the next mutually agreed time to talk about romance, it stops him from procrastinating indefinitely or allowing him the excuse that he just hasn't got around to it yet because he hasn't had enough time. By setting another appointment he has a deadline to work towards. Secondly, it also gives a set time for an analysis of how romance has been going in the relationship. There may need to be a little more initiation or thought on behalf of the man or a reminder of some of the main points you talked to him about. It also gives a time for an assessment of the benefits to him. Thirdly, it gives a further opportunity for you to verbalise your appreciation of his efforts, which will encourage him further in his attempts at romance. A follow up date that positively conveys how happy you are with his efforts at being romantic will in itself act as a self-propelling fuel for his romantic gestures.

Fourthly, it will also help him not to take for granted the benefits he has enjoyed from romance verbalised and listed on this occasion as they are reinforced and underlined before him. Don't let him take the benefits for granted. Get him to verbalise them for himself so that he does in fact understand that the benefits are real. If you have a product to sell a customer (in this case romance), get them to verbalise for themselves all the benefits they have received because they now use this product. By getting your man to say, "Yes, I really have enjoyed... making you happy... seeing the surprise on your face when I produced those flowers for you... seeing you so contented... making love the way we did after that special romantic dinner... the way I have been feeling about us lately", etc., you are in effect getting him to agree that romance is a great thing for your relationship. You are underlining and emphasising the benefits by his own words rather than by your own words. Finally, by arranging this follow up date you are also injecting another romantic time together into your relationship. This can be important to keep that romantic snowball rolling ahead.

The main objective of this chapter is for you to get your man to have a positive ***attitude*** to romance. There is the old saying that says, "You can lead a horse to water but you can't get it to drink". You must get your man to have a positive attitude towards romance so that he will want to drink, indeed so that you won't be able to hold him back. You can try and change a person's actions by all sorts of means but they will, in the long run, all prove to be ineffective and futile. But if a person has the same attitude as yourself, if he is won over to approach the topic with the same presuppositions and starting point, then you have won the battle already. Develop in your man a strong positive attitude to romance and you will be the envy of many a woman.

Develop in your man a strong positive attitude to romance and you will be the envy of many a woman.

SUMMARY OF CHAPTER FIVE

Firstly, make sure your communication is excellent.

Invite your man to a special date.

> Choose the time carefully.
> Choose the venue carefully.
> Advertise it as being beneficial to both of you.

On the date

> Start with your list of questions for you both to answer
> Outline the benefits for him.
> Be positive.
> Remind him of his romantic acts in the past and how these made you feel.
> Don't be disagreeable.
> Remove any barriers that may stop him from being a romantic.
> Get a commitment from him.
> Give him a romantic name to live up to.
> Look for what provides him with the best incentive.
> Stroke his male ego with his romantic nature.
> Help him understand romance for a woman is like sex to a man.
> Don't dominate the discussion but get him to respond to your ideas and let him think about creating his own romantic ideas.
> Once you get a commitment from him don't go on and on but

talk about the things he wants to talk about.

After the date
Let your man experience the benefits of romance first hand.
Arrange a follow up date so that -
It sets a time frame for him to begin to be more romantic.
You have a set time to analyse how romance has grown in the relationship since the first date.
You can verbalise your appreciation of his efforts.
He doesn't take for granted the benefits he has enjoyed.
You inject another romantic time into your relationship.

The main objective is to get your man to have a positive attitude towards romance.

6

CHAPTER SIX

KEEPING A GOOD THING GOING

"(Kids) don't remember what you try to teach them. They remember what you are." (Jim Henson, It's Not Easy Being Green: And Other Things To Consider)

So your man has embraced the idea of being a romantic. He understands your need for it, the benefits for him and what romance is, but can you realistically expect him to continue to keep the flame of romance burning brightly forever? While it depends upon your man to carry the flame for romance in your relationship by initiating romance and having the proper attitude towards it, the fuel on which the candle burns can be increased by yourself. By this I mean that you will have to encourage, reward and remind your mate about romance. You are the one that can make sure that your relationship doesn't run out of fuel so that your romantic love can keep burning even if it is stoked by your spouse. Someone once said, "We need to be reminded more than we need to be taught", and this is true. The secret however, is how to remind without nagging, how to remind him without you feeling as if you have to prod him every time you want there to be romance in your relationship.

How to continue romance in your relationship is just as important as educating your man or getting a romantic commitment from him. Different things work better for some people than others, so make sure you discover what things work best for you and your man and then keep those things up. If something works well then keep the formula going. On the other hand, you have to realise that there is often more than just one type of fuel on which a romantic flame will burn. Throughout this chapter we will look at different ideas to keep romance alive in your relationship and keep your man a romantic for the rest of his life. Use the ideas that work for you but don't be afraid to try new ones.

Inject Premarital Behaviour Into Your Relationship

It doesn't matter whether you are married or whether you have been together for an extended period. The point is that relationships can lose their zest over time. It is often said that romance only lasts during courtship and the first eighteen months or so of marriage.[7] Part of this can be attributed to the "newness" of the relationship. There is a lot to learn about the other; discovery is exciting and romantic. But what happens when you think you know all there is to know about your man and maybe wish you didn't; or at least wished to make some changes? Can "newness" be part of an old relationship? Yes it can, by making some small, new changes to the routine of your relationship. Intimate relationships can easily fall into a trap of just existence instead of excitement, but by injecting things into your relationship like what you did before you became serious, you can relive that excitement, and that newness. Think back to the things you and your spouse did in the early stages of the relationship. Where did you go and what did you do together? By taking time to do these things again, by going to those places again, you are reliving and focusing on that most romantic time of your lives.

You can still do new things in an old relationship and it will result in romance. Just as long as both parties enjoy it and it is done together. You may like to experiment by doing new things together, which you may not have done during the early stages of your relationship. The main point is that you inject premarital behaviour into your lives. Go out to the movies again, eat out, go to a park and be pushed on a swing, enjoy the frivolity of amusement centres, walk along the beach. Just get out of the house, communicate and be with the man that you chose to love forever. Talk and listen. Draw out your mate's feelings when you walk through a park, walk along the beach or go for a drive. The important thing is that you slow down and make time for the two of you to do nothing but go out in a new environment and connect. Give time for your relationship to be nurtured. It won't happen usually unless you plan for it. Make such times that both of you enjoy part of your routine so that it becomes a good habit for both of you.

For those couples who are serious about romance and nurturing their relationship, I suggest they set aside one night a week, which is committed purely to the growth of their relationship. It can be spent in different activities each week but can involve what I call "super quality time". "Super quality time" is time spent, which charges the relationship with romantic power. It involves activities such as talking about your dreams and hopes, expressing your love for each other, expressing how much your partner means to you, appreciation and admiration, affirmation of your commitment to the relationship and your expression of continued attraction to your partner. Imagine the changes if this practice was followed in every intimate relationship. Unfortunately, in many relationships, these things are never verbalised from one year to the next and then people wonder why romance eludes them in their relationships! Yet when many people first begin to become romantically involved they include a measure of these "super quality times".

> *"Super quality time" is time spent, which charges the relationship with romantic power.*

Were you ever adventurous enough in the earlier (probably more romantic) stages of your relationship to be seen together embracing or kissing for long periods in public places? Did you ever make love in a car, outdoors or motel? Why not try the same again and relive your earlier enjoyable experiences? The world of opportunities has not changed. Romance is everywhere if you start to look for it. Indeed once you look through romantic glasses just about everywhere and anything can present with opportunities for romance.

Role Reversal Dates

Warren Farrell explains the role reversal date and its virtues. He concludes, "It's also an amazing turn on".[8] Although not necessarily a new idea, role reversal or insight reversal can allow both partners the view from the other side of the fence. It can also release the tensions of conforming to stereotypes, if you allow yourself to take on your partner's role during a date. How it works is like this.

You explain to your man how on this one occasion you will act out the traditional male role and he will act out the traditional female role. You organise the date, you drive the car, you pay the bill and you make passes at **him** all evening. On the other hand, he acts out or can even exaggerate the female role by listening attentively, acting coy, especially when a pass is made at him, plays down anything overtly sexual and just has a really good time.

The whole idea of this date is to get out of the normal routine of a stereotyped date and allow each partner to undo some of the ruts the relationship may be falling into.⁹ It can be fun and exciting to step out of your own role and play someone else's role. If you are a passive person you can allow yourself the pleasure of acting out a more aggressive role. You can also show your man what it is like to be a real romantic that maybe he can imitate when you reverse back again. Go out and try it. If your mate likes it and you both can handle it then suggest it again sometime.

Another different type of date is to simulate meeting for the first time. The idea behind this is for both of you to arrive at a certain place, for instance a restaurant, but not together. You may arrive ten minutes apart but make it look to everyone as if you have just met for the first time. How you actually get together and introduce yourselves can be either planned or spontaneous. Your man may wish to pay you compliments, or vice versa, through a third person (for example, a waiter or waitress), convincing them, of course, that he doesn't know you, but would like to. Being paid these compliments through the medium of a third person can be quite stimulating as well as being very romantic. Acting out meeting each other for the first time and "asking basic questions about values, what they do and want out of life", helps to bring a couple back to basics. "The process helps a couple remember why they chose each other, and to feel acutely how deep the loss of the other would be. When we fear loss most, changing is put into perspective before it is too late".¹⁰

Being paid these compliments through the medium of a third person can be quite stimulating as well as being very romantic.

Start a Romantic Message Pad

Do you wish your man would leave you romantic messages on a regular basis? By starting a romantic message pad, you can create the circumstances to make the means available to your man. All you do is buy a whiteboard or some other device on which you can write and rewrite messages on. The only rule is that it is to be used for no other purpose than romantic messages to and from your spouse. If you have bills to pay or other messages then give them another home. Don't let them ever be allowed on your special message board. You may wish to even impose a romantic penalty if your spouse does happen to disobey this rule. It may be something like him owing you a massage or dinner date or him cooking dinner (if he doesn't usually do the cooking).

Make sure you can keep your special romantic pad in a central place where both of you can read it and be reminded of it. By writing special love notes of a romantic nature and by encouraging your man to do the same, you are verbalising your feelings to your partner in a different medium and you create the atmosphere and attitude of romance. Verbalising your love for your spouse also helps *you* get in touch with those feelings. The same will be true with your mate. As he writes down romantic feelings he has towards you the more he will understand and get in touch with those feelings. It is like when you are trying to learn and remember some information for an exam. Often the best way to make sure you understand something is to relate it in full to another person. If you have difficulty in one area, when relating the information to another you become aware that that particular area is the one you have lost touch with. So it is with relating feelings to our loved ones. By verbalising them to others, it underlines them in our own minds and reminds us how important they really are.

> *By writing special love notes of a romantic nature and by encouraging your man to do the same, you are verbalising your feelings to your partner in a different medium and you create the atmosphere and attitude of romance.*

Get A Romantic Glamour Photo Of Yourself

This is an idea that is sure to add glamour to your relationship. A glamour shot is where you are glamorised by make-up and backdrops and then photographed by a professional photographer. The subject is often photographed in lingerie or something sexy with a variety of poses. Then when the photo shoot is over you can pick out which one you wish to enlarge. Alternatively you may wish for your mate to choose, seeing it will be for him. Don't write this idea off too early as there are a lot of advantages for both you and him. Sure, you may be a little embarrassed about being photographed in lingerie in provocative poses. But it will be for your man and, although it might sound naughty, it could also be a whole lot of fun. There are a lot of professional photographers who specialise solely in glamour photos and make you feel right at home. Even if you are not sold on the idea, visit a studio and talk over the ideas with the photographer. Getting to know the person first can help and they (he/she) should be able to show you a whole album of "before and after" shots of previously taken photographs. No matter how plain you may think yourself, these professionals can make you look like a million dollars. But after all, isn't that what you and your mate deserve, to see you looking your best?

If you are a little shy about having a glamour photo of yourself in lingerie enlarged and framed, remember that it is not for the whole world to see - only for you and your man. You will not be hanging it in a public place but in your private bedroom where a lot of other very private things take place. Hanging the photo in your bedroom will give the room a romantic atmosphere so that even when you may not feel or look glamorous, both you and your man are reminded of how desirable you really are.

If anyone in a sexy negligee is going to stimulate your man you want it to be you. So don't be afraid to show a little leg, swell, cleavage or whatever you feel comfortable with, just make it sexy and enjoy it. Once hanging on the wall of your bedroom it also serves as a romantic reminder of your involvement with, and love for, each other. With such a picture hanging in your bedroom how could it be anything but a romantic room ever again?

Once hanging on the wall of your bedroom a glamour photo also serves as a romantic reminder of your involvement with, and love for, each other.

You may like to surprise your man with the photo by giving it to him as a gift for his birthday for instance. Alternatively you may wish for him to be part of it from the very beginning by attending the shooting of the photograph at the studio and choosing, or helping to choose, which photo will be enlarged and framed.

If he is willing he may prefer to pose for one himself, either with you or by himself. Here you can have some input as to how you would like him dressed (or undressed) so you can have your own glamour photograph of him. You might also prefer to have a number of smaller photos of you both in a romantic collage. It's all your choice.

Start a Romantic Money Box

Just as your romantic message board is exclusively for romantic messages, so a romantic money box will be exclusively for romantic gifts and outings. You can either have a joint money box or individual ones. The amount of money that is deposited is not the main point of the romantic money box. The main point is that you have a collection spot that can remind and stimulate you both to think of ideas to spend this romantic money. You may wish to start an actual separate bank account but remember that this will not be as visible as a money box and it will not always be as practical to deposit lose change into.

The main point is that you have a collection spot that can remind and stimulate you both to think of ideas to spend this romantic money.

Don't be alarmed that this will interfere with your budget, as it does not need to be large amounts. Imagine a few dollars a week. That could possibly be used by your mate to buy you a bunch of flowers every few weeks. That's many times throughout the year! How much improvement would that be on the present? The money box is also a great problem solver when one partner argues that there is no money to go out to dinner tonight. Because the romantic money box cannot be used for other purposes, it can be used for such events.

Encourage your mate to contribute to the romantic money box and also encourage him to let you see him adding to it. It is very easy for him to exaggerate in his own mind how many times he contributes to the money box, when you ask him. But if he is encouraged that his partner is pleased and happy when she sees him adding to the money box he will be more likely to do so. Something else you can do to remind him without actually telling him is to get him to actually drop in your contributions. By giving him a few cents while you are busy, and asking him to go and place the coins in the money box, you are bringing it to his attention and he is actually manually completing the action required to contribute to the cause. By giving him small amounts you remove the possibility of him complaining about it being too large a contribution.

Too often our money is spent on the mortgage repayments and the (so-called) expenses of living. It can be great watching the money grow but the real fun comes when you can spend the contents of the romantic money box on yourselves without feeling guilty about robbing it from another area of your budget.

Start a Romantic Diary

A good thing about a romantic diary is that you don't have to necessarily write in it every day. The idea of keeping a romantic diary is to record all the different romantic things that happen between the two of you. It can record something you or your partner does for the other, it can record feelings, reactions, appreciation, expectations and goals. A romantic diary in itself can actually increase romance through several ways.

Firstly, it reminds you of how romantic your man has been. It's easy to forget little acts of romance but recording them in a diary reserved just for romance can bring all those fond memories back again. Make sure you always keep your diary positive so that it will be romantic and never disappointing. Then when you read it, even if you are feeling a bit blue beforehand, you will be invigorated with positive romance.

Something else that a romantic diary does is to remind you to encourage his attempts. As you read the pages of your diary you will be reminded of all the romantic things your spouse has done for you. When they are gathered together they can fill you with appreciation for your mate. It is important to encourage his attempts if you want him to continue to be a romantic.

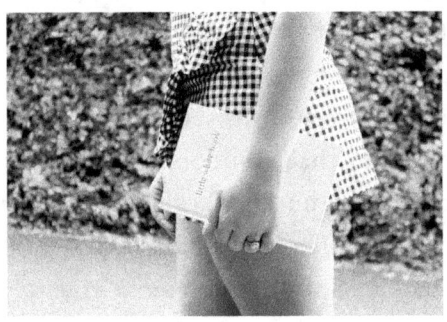

Furthermore, a romantic diary will provide you with the facts you need to analyse your methods and how they have worked. By recording what things you have done and what response your spouse has taken, you can see what areas provide the best and enduring romantic behaviour from your man.

Finally, a romantic diary also keeps romance fresh and central in your mind. As you record events and feelings in the diary it helps to keep romance high on your list of priorities. Then when you read it, it can also enthuse you to try new ideas and keep romance alive because you can see the value of romance. You can use it to review the years but also to list goals and see how those goals are being attained. You can see what projects you have spent your money on from your romantic money box and remind yourself of little things that you would have long forgotten if they had not been recorded. A romantic diary can add romance in itself, and can preserve vivid memories of a life time of romantic loving.

> *A romantic diary can add romance in itself, and can preserve vivid memories of a life time of romantic loving.*

Award Him A Romantic Trophy

One of the good points about the romantic money box is that it provides a reminder for romance without you actively saying or doing anything. It just sits there and even if it doesn't collect fortunes it provides a constant reminder whenever it is seen. This is a silent reminder that is just what you want so that you don't have to verbally remind him or be accused of nagging. Another excellent reminder is what I call the "romantic trophy award". The idea is for you to go to a shop that sells trophies and purchase an appropriate one to give to your man. The inscription on the plaque should read, "World Champion Romantic", or something similar. A lot of trophies have figurines of various sports on them so you may have to get one especially made or maybe just buy a trophy without a figurine.

If you placed in your family room a sign that read, "I want you to be a romantic man" or "you must be more romantic", your man would probably take the sign down, accuse you of nagging, complain aggressively and probably wish to never be romantic again. It would be a type of scolding that would probably initiate the opposite type of behaviour you are seeking. If, however, your man has a trophy saying how good he is at something, it can only encourage him, remind him of his romantic nature and give him the romantic name you want him to have and live up to. That is a type of positive reinforcement that builds desire to live up to those expectations.

Once you have bought the trophy you may wish to wait until your man makes some romantic effort and then present it to him telling him how much he deserves it. There are a few variations you can make depending on how much you like the idea and, more importantly, how much he likes the idea. There are not too many people in this world who don't like to receive trophies. Instead of making it "world champion" you can just put your town, state or country. Then after his romantic efforts improve you can either get another plaque to add to the trophy or buy a whole new trophy to show how his title has enlarged. Other variations can include changes to the title itself, such as "champion romantic lover", or "Champion Romantic Partner". Variations are only limited to your imagination; however, I have purposely kept the root word, "romance" in each example. Remember it is the romance that you wish him to be reminded of and enforced every time he looks at his impressive trophy.

> *There are not too many people in this world who don't like to receive trophies.*

Having such a trophy on display will also occasionally capture your visitors' interest as well. This will also act as another reminder but will also mean he will have a romantic name to live up to in their eyes. Visitors may see it as humorous but you can come to his rescue by saying how he deserves it and how no other man comes up to his standard. This will save your man playing down the trophy and its significance but will also stroke his male ego. Who is he going to be to argue that other men don't come up to his standard in intimate relationships?

Certainly the effect of the trophy will be more significant if your man has no other trophies on display. If on the other hand, your man has scores of trophies everywhere, another one may lose its effect. In this case for it to keep on working long past the day it is presented, you will have to make the trophy "stand out" from the crowd in some way. It may be size, shape, colour or type but it will have to attract attention over all the others.

Provide The Environment To Enhance Romance

No matter how hard he tries, your man is not going to be Mr Romance wearing either old pyjamas with the draw string hanging out, or old Y-front undies with the elastic stretched. Neither will *you* feel like Mrs Romance if your nightie is old and torn or unexciting. Search through your man's wardrobe and assess how romantic are his underclothes and nightwear. You may need to go shopping for both him and yourself to buy a couple of garments that make you both feel romantic and sexy. The feeling you will feel and the atmosphere you will set will be well worth the cost of a few dollars. Even if you are not used to wearing anything to bed you can still buy some lingerie and start wearing it well *before* bedtime. Stretch out this most romantic part of the day and you can possibly feel romantic even before he comes home. This sets an atmosphere in itself rather than your man only ever seeing your night wear immediately when you change to go to bed. It is important that you do everything you possibly can to help you both feel romantic and also to remove any unromantic barriers. Even a pauper can look like a prince if he is bathed, shaved, clothed like a prince and given a throne. Dress romantically and look romantic, and you both will be more likely to *feel* romantic.

> **Stretch out this most romantic part of the day and you can possibly feel romantic even before he comes home.**

Unfortunately, we often wonder why we don't feel like a princess when the problem is that our royal bed chamber is unkempt. Remember that a romantic bedroom is a tidy one. Often junk can accumulate in the bedroom faster than anywhere else. If we are worried about visitors seeing a mess we often transfer it to the bedroom, treating it as a storeroom. But where does it go from there? There's nothing like a room full of junk to make you depressed, which in turn can stop you from feeling romantic. Try your best to keep it neat and notice the difference.

Another extra romantic touch is to have satin sheets. Not everybody loves them so make sure your man approves of the feel before you outlay such a cost. If you can't afford the expense, try purchasing just the pillowcases first. In this way you can still feel that silky feeling at least around your face for only a fraction of the cost of the full bed set. Then if you really love the feel, you can save for the rest of the set.

Look around your bedroom and see what romantic touches you can add. Remember that this is the most romantic room of your home so give it the care and attention it deserves. Paint a romantic background and you are more likely to have a total romantic picture. Get all of the smaller details romantic, all of the ones that lie in your power to change, and you will provide the atmosphere that will greatly influence the total picture towards romance.

Highlight Past Romantic Experiences The Two Of You Have Shared Together

Highlighting past romantic experiences can remind a man of how romantic he has been in the past, as well as reminding him of the topic of romance in general. You can do this in a variety of ways. Firstly, make a list of all the romantic things you have done together in the past and then talk about them. Reminding your partner of the romantic occasions, scenes and actions in the past history of your relationship, can help to recapture those times. We don't remember past experiences on only one level or with only one sense. One of the great things about memories is that we can often remember the feeling, seeing, hearing, tasting, smelling or responses of other people to past occasions. We can relive those memories in our minds again and again.

By reminding ourselves and our spouse about them we can share that experience with them again. It is sometimes difficult to explain a memory to someone else unless they have been there too. Maybe you have had the experience of going back to a house you used to live in and have experienced the memory of the sense of living there again. All sorts of feelings can be relived in this way. By triggering warm, romantic feelings of the past, you can not only remind but also enthuse your spouse to carry on those feelings into the present.

But how do you refer to romantic memories without becoming a broken record and annoying your mate? A good way is not just to bring up a memory out of the blue without any "lead in" to the conversation. You should provide the romantic memory with a joining link to the present situation. For example, you can say, "That reminds me when you..." or, "That was just like when we..." In this way you can continue the theme of your conversation without a blunt interruption of the topic. If you can get your man to respond to those romantic memories positively, by getting him to contribute to the recall of the memory, you will also allow him to relive the memory more vividly with you.

Looking through old photo albums is another way of recapturing past romantic occasions. Photos of holidays or before you were living together, can be a treasure chest of precious memories and fun times. Wedding photos themselves are also important. If you are married, how often have you and your man looked through your wedding photos together after you initially received them? Weddings and everything connected with them are extremely romantic occasions. They formalise and symbolise love, total commitment, the giving of oneself, romance, youthfulness, family connections, the beginning of a new life together, celebration, exciting new experiences and probably a hundred other romantic themes. That is why it is good for both partners to occasionally be reminded by looking again at their wedding photos. Even other peoples' weddings can be romantic for you and your man, the more you share the occasion with them. Don't be afraid to participate or help in the preparation of weddings especially if you can get your man involved with you.

Finally, you can also highlight past romantic experiences even if they are not personally attributed to you. Referring to other peoples' romantic gestures can also impart a contagious spirit upon your man if you explain the feelings of the people concerned. Explain how inventive the romantic act was, how exhilarated the woman must have felt or how the man's actions typified the kind of man every woman only ever dreams of. You can also elaborate on how much pleasure the man received or how it was a turn-on for both partners.

When referring to romantic experiences other than your own, make sure you don't include your own personal opinions directly but make the comments in the third person. Instead of saying, "I think it would have been beautiful", say, "It must have been beautiful", or "I'm sure she felt..." Don't leave room for feelings of jealousy by including your own personal desires of the man involved, or his actions. By making your observations neutral, or expressing what the other party felt, you don't leave room for your man to believe you are implicitly ridiculing him or comparing him with anyone else (a hard act to follow). By explicitly saying to your man, "You never do that", you would be comparing him to someone else for the purpose of exposing his shortfall. That is a good way to get people on the defensive immediately and to oppose your personal attacks. But staying neutral will mean that he is free to make any comparisons, draw any conclusions he wants to, in his own time, without being condemned or told to change by the woman he loves.

Introduce A Back Scratching Agreement

The old saying, "You scratch my back and I'll scratch yours" is the catch phrase of a relationship that benefits both parties. In an intimate relationship there is give and take, fulfil and be fulfilled. But you cannot fulfil desires and needs unless you know for sure what they are. So there needs to be open communication and education about our needs, their needs and how to fulfil them. Unfortunately we often don't do exactly that, and so desires remain unfulfilled and frustration results.

What I have called the "back scratching agreement" is where you and your man each write down a certain number of things you wish you had more of in your relationship. Then, of course, you swap the lists and both of you try fulfilling the other's wishes for the next week. This agreement can do three things. It can clarify real needs from things a person merely *thought* were really important but realises now that they don't matter that much. It also provides another avenue to direct, express and educate real needs, which is especially helpful if your man finds it hard to express his emotions verbally. Finally, it allows a way of getting the needs of both partners met at the same time.

Don't Always Expect To Be The Receiver

"One way to bring romance back into your life is by doing something romantic for your man".[11] Although romance is to be initiated by the man you can always stimulate and encourage him by occasionally being the giver rather than the receiver of romance. Try pampering him sometime without expecting a reciprocal act. Give him a massage, scrub his back when he bathes or sit at his feet and rub them if he likes that. Buy him a special gift not because it is his birthday or Christmas but "just because". By doing something romantic for your man you are in fact being involved in romantic behaviour. Not only is this a good feeling in itself (being a romantic giver) but it does tend to encourage reciprocal behaviour in your spouse. Human nature is such that we do feel obliged when people do things for us. When people give us Christmas gifts it is natural to feel we should give them a gift as well. Whether it is pride or a sense of fairness, we often feel as if we should repay kindness that is given without conditions. However, if kindness is given in such a way that it is seen as manipulative or a reciprocal act is to be expected, then it is worthless and can engender resentment. So when you do something romantic, do it with no strings attached and there will be more of a chance that he will return it anyway.

Cultivate Friendship

The basis of all good, happy relationships is friendship. The marriage relationship and intimate relationships in general are no exception. In all relationships, friendship is cultivated by common ground, areas in which both parties feel comfortable and enjoy. In intimate relationships, this common ground is called compatibility. A couple are called compatible if they share common interests, values, desires, backgrounds, etc.

Unfortunately after years of long term intimate relationships people sometimes don't cultivate the friendship area of their relationship and they tend to move in different directions. Spouses can move apart from each other often by developing interests outside the common ground areas or to the exclusion of common ground.

> *Spouses can move apart from each other often by developing interests outside the common ground areas or to the exclusion of common ground.*

It can also be triggered by one or both partners not sharing the same friendship circles. This happens when close or many friends are made by one spouse but not shared with the other. By sharing common friends with our spouses we don't begin living in different worlds that can act to separate us. Think about the number of friends that you have and then in turn the friends of your man. Then work out how many of them are common to both of you. There will of course be a percentage of friends who will not be common to both of you because they will be related to work or other areas.

I have devised an exercise for you to determine the percentage of common friendship you share with your spouse. Fill out the list on the left-hand side while you get your man to list his closest friends on another piece of paper. When finished there may be some friends that either of you have forgotten, which the other listed. In this case compare the lists and add any forgotten names. Then add your spouse's list next to yours and work out the number of friends that are shared. You can then make this a percentage figure by multiplying the number of shared friends by one hundred and dividing this by the total number of friends of your partner. Thus the formula looks like this:

$$\frac{\text{Number of shared friends}}{\text{Number of partner's friends}} \times \frac{100}{1} = \text{\% of shared friends}$$

Here is an example:

Your man's list   Your list

Total   24   Total 10
Number shared 6   Number shared 6
% Shared =   25%   % Shared =   60%

You will notice that although the number of friends shared will always be the same, the percentage between the partners can change dramatically because of the difference in the totals. That is why it is important to agree on the definition of what constitutes a close friend, and for both partners to check each other's list. In the example I have used above you can see how there is a considerable difference between the two percentages. A vast difference in percentages, or two low percentages can indicate a tendency to grow apart. You can see it diagrammatically by marking your own two percentages below.

0 10 20 30 40 50 60 70 80 90 100
Growing apart   Growing together

You can quickly work out whether the bulk of you or your man's friends are robbing you of common friendship. If so, then you may need to cultivate common friendship that will increase your time of togetherness. Don't let the excessively time consuming friendship of a girlfriend your man cannot stand, stop the togetherness of you and your man. On the other hand, you may wish to try to make new friendships which both you and your man can share.

If your friendship area with your spouse is lacking somewhat, then try injecting fun times into it. Often in long term relationships people can become so busy working for the financial needs or the responsible side of the relationship that they forget how to have simple fun being friends. Intimate relationships can provide limitless areas over which to argue - including roles, spending money (which you may or may not have), priorities, child discipline, in-laws, power balance and chores. Is it any wonder that there can remain little time to develop and cultivate friendships that are so important?

> *Often in long term relationships people can become so busy working for the financial needs or the responsible side of the relationship that they forget how to have simple fun being friends.*

Your best friends are people you want to spend all of your time with and you enjoy their presence. They can share fun times with you but they are also there for you in the hard times. Friendship requires common ground but also time. Remember to inject quality time into your relationship so that your partner is your best friend, not just a roommate that really lives in a different world to you. Connect with your partner through friendship and romance will follow naturally.

SUMMARY OF CHAPTER SIX

Inject premarital behaviour into your lives.
Try a role reversal date.
Try acting as if you are meeting for the first time.
Start a romantic message pad.
Get a romantic glamour photo of yourself, and maybe him, or both together.
Start a romantic money box.
Start a romantic diary.
Award him a romantic trophy.
Provide the environment to enhance romance. Use sexy lingerie and keep the bedroom tidy and sensual.

Highlight past romantic experiences that the two of you have shared together.

Introduce a back scratching agreement. Communicate wishes and fulfil them.

Don't always expect to be the receiver. Do something romantic for your man.

Cultivate friendship. Increase common friends and grow together. Inject fun times and quality times into your friendship with your spouse.

CHAPTER SEVEN

ROMANCE - THE TWO EDGED SWORD

"There are two basic motivating forces: fear and love. When we are afraid, we pull back from life. When we are in love, we open to all that life has to offer with passion, excitement and acceptance." (John Lennon)

Let's summarise a couple of the concepts we've learned so far before we get into an area that can be very challenging. Firstly, we have stated that romance is a need for a woman. We also have said that romance is an aphrodisiac for a woman. Keeping this in mind, we need to be aware of several forces that seek to sabotage desire, romance and pleasure especially targeted at women. Firstly, we need to consider some of the sexual history facts which have had a major impact on how desire, romance and pleasure is viewed and inhibited today. You may be quick to respond that the history of sex doesn't affect *my* ability to experience pleasure, desire or romance today but don't be so quick to make such a snap judgement without considering the facts. It is also important to realise that the information you are about to consider often works at a level far below consciousness. In other words, these forces work subconsciously on you without you even being aware of it happening. That is why it is so insidious. That is why other things often get the blame for the destructive havoc wrought by these forces.

The history of the Christian church of inhibiting desire and sexuality is very confronting. Very early on in its history it was men in positions of religious power and control who insisted on inhibiting all forms of sexual pleasure. Yes, you heard it right, all forms of sexual pleasure. They very early on insisted that sexuality and spirituality could not occupy the same space. These two concepts were mutually exclusive and opposed to each other. If one was to be spiritual then one could not be sexual in any way. Now you could say that everyone is welcome to their opinion, even if they are completely wrong so why should that matter much at all. Indeed some people today have the most wackiest of ideas but everyone else knows it so why should that be a concern? The problem was that these men thought they spoke on behalf of God himself, and most of the people back then believed that also. The church soon became a political as well as a religious power which meant it had total power. When it came to have absolute power it also enforced it absolutely, even to go so far as to enforce the death penalty for minor infringements of its copious laws.

At the heart of the matter was the church's incorrect teaching that pleasure was sinful. The church very soon failed to integrate sexuality with spirituality. This failure resulted in sexuality becoming the enemy. One early Christian leader by the name of Origen (185-254AD) was so vehemently opposed to sexuality that he castrated himself! It was Jerome (347-420AD) another great in the early Christian church who taught that all sex was impure. Later Augustine (354-430AD) who had a major influence on religious thought, taught that sex was tolerated only for procreation otherwise it was sin. The punchline however, was that he added sex was sin ***especially if there was pleasure involved!***

At the heart of the matter was the church's incorrect teaching that pleasure was sinful.

But wait it gets worse. It was Theodore in the 7th century who drew up a penitence list where premeditated murder got seven years, however, wait for it, oral sex got seven years to life! Several hundred years later during the dark ages in the 13th century it was the church's "Codex Latinus Monacensis" that stated a wife's agreement to deviate from the missionary position was as serious as murder. Notice how the burden of guilt was placed upon the woman. It wasn't so much that the couple were to be punished. It was when the *wife* agreed to deviate from the one and only church-endorsed position (only to conceive children mind you) that a terrible sin was declared. Of course in addition to this there were prescribed periods of church enforced abstinence totalling five months per year. Celibacy was soon seen as of higher value than marriage and virginity was the ultimate prized state. The 12th century saw the rise of the veneration of worship of the virgin Mary. The church brought a hatred of pleasure. It outlawed pleasure and made it a sin. It is because of this historical concept that sex was tolerated only for procreation that the Catholic Church still maintains such a hard anti-contraceptive stance. You simply must not have sex for pleasure (and free of the stress of the risk of pregnancy). Every time you have sex you must be trying to make another Catholic. It is further interesting that even after the reformation occurred, many protestant religions still kept the catholic concepts linking guilt and sin with sex. When missionaries visited the islands of the pacific for example, the "Missionary" position became known and taught as the "proper" and only position to have sex.

This hatred of pleasure that the church brought in and ingrained in populations for nearly two thousand years was in complete contrast to the teachings of both the Old Testament and the New Testament on which the religion was based. The Jewish religion (which recognises the Old Testament) for instance, promoted a healthy sexuality in stark contrast to Catholic teachings. The book in the Bible known as Song Of Solomon was an erotic piece of literature between a couple full of desire and sexuality. Notice the following quotes from the book found in the middle of the Bible.

> *This hatred of pleasure that the church brought in and ingrained in populations for nearly two thousand years was in complete contrast to the teachings of both the old testament and the new testament on which the religion was based.*

"Let her breasts satisfy you at all times and always be enraptured with her love." (5:19 NKJV) "Let him kiss me with the kisses of his mouth – for your love is better than wine." (1:2 NKJV) "I sat down in his shade with great delight, and his fruit was sweet to my taste." (2:3 NKJV) "His left hand is under my head, and his right hand embraces me." (2:6 NKJV) As Joseph Dillow points out most Hebrew scholars agree that the word used here for "embrace" actually means to stimulate sexually or fondle.[12] "How fair and how pleasant you are, o love, with your delights! This statue of yours is like a palm tree, and your breasts like its clusters. I said, "I will go up to the palm tree, I will take hold of its branches." Let now your breasts be like clusters of the vine, the fragrance of your breath like apples, and the roof of your mouth like the best wine." (7:6-9 NKJV)

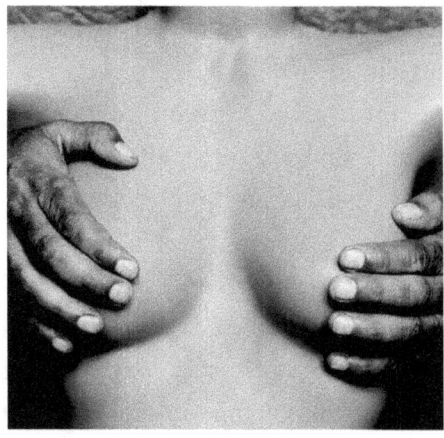

There are many more that could be quoted but you get the idea. Some Hebrew scholars also insist there are references to oral sex in the book. But then you turn to the New Testament and there are also recorded there healthy discourses on sexual relationships. "So husbands should love their own wives as their own bodies" (Ephesians 5:28 NKJV), "... and the two shall become one flesh" (Ephesians 5:31 NKJV) and "Marriage is honourable among all, and the bed undefiled" (Hebrews 13:4 NKJV), all three from St Paul himself. When you put both testaments together you find the number one relationship throughout the whole bible that is repeatedly compared to the relationship God wants with humans is the sexual relationship. For example, "And as the bridegroom rejoices over the bride, so shall your God rejoice over you." (Isaiah 62:5 NKJV) So there is all this desire, intimacy, romance and expectation in the Bible and yet the church has killed it all off and made it a sin. There has been a conspiracy. God actually invented sex. The one word chosen by the bible to describe God is love. The clitoris is the only organ that is designed for pleasure and if you do take the biblical approach, this was God's intention. But Christianity is not the only religion which has had its teachings misconstrued in an attempt to minimise pleasure in sexuality. Some other religious groups have resulted in the barbaric removal of the female clitoris in female babies with the direct attempt to stop all sexual pleasure in the future woman. C S Lewis says it best when he says "Of all evil men, religious evil men are the worst." It seems from many different religious fronts women's pleasure has been assaulted over and over again.

So what is the point in all of this you might say? Here is the point. If you have had even a subtle influence from this dark ages teaching that sex, pleasure and desire is sin, then you will have some sort of inhibition happening in your sexuality. Whether you were taught at a Catholic school and went to church every Sunday, whether there were just rigid beliefs about sex in your family of origin or whether you have just picked up guilt, low self-esteem or other negative vague references that you shouldn't be enjoying pleasure, they will all be exerting a strong force upon you to try and stop you experiencing pleasure, romance and desire from your intimate relationship.

If you have had even a subtle influence from this dark ages teaching that sex, pleasure and desire is sin, then you will have some sort of inhibition happening in your sexuality.

GUILT

Guilt has many manifestations. Many women do not enjoy sex or intimacy, others have diminished orgasms and others can't get aroused and yet none of them realise that guilt is often the culprit.

"Guilt like shame is a powerful anti-aphrodisiac. Whereas shame is a feeling that the self is defective, guilt involves a sense that the self needs to be punished... A common form of guilt-induced self-punishment is to remove sexual pleasure from one's life. If this process is unconscious, then the individual only knows that she/he isn't enjoying sex, not that she/he requires one's self not to enjoy it."[13] The fact of the matter is that there are untold millions of women who are not enjoying their sexuality due to the feelings of guilt they carry. The actual guilt causes are endless, from a harsh word from an authority figure or parent, a look of disapproval of how one is dressed, a refusal to accept a new spouse by a parent, a sexual tryst or one night stand that went wrong, a feeling of unworthiness, a low self-esteem, a difficult opposite sex parent relationship - any one cause can result in a woman punishing herself through denying or minimising pleasure in her life. A good mantra for every woman is therefore "I am worthy". Worthy to receive pleasure. Worthy to enjoy love. Worthy to be loved. Worthy to enjoy intimacy and worthy to have as many earth shattering orgasms as you want.

Guilt programs sexual responses in many varied ways. Widow guilt for instance programs a woman so that she can never have a sexual relationship with a man again without feeling tremendous guilt at being disloyal to her dead partner. Some other relationships start in an atmosphere of guilt. It might be some illicit affair where guilt is involved. The guilt then gets associated with adrenaline. Once this adrenaline-guilt connection is made and reinforced then sexual experiences that lack the adrenaline-guilt connection become too mundane to tolerate and the person moves from one relationship to another looking for the same high they got from a previous guilt ridden one. Another way guilt programs sexuality and sexual responses is found in rigid anti-sex teaching. "Nice girls don't..." becomes an inhibitory force that minimises orgasms or banishes them completely. Guilt can further be responsible for discomfort with involuntary sexual responses such as facial grimaces, foot spasms and any verbal responses such as moans and groans. All of these guilt-induced inhibitory responses work to deny pleasure in a woman's life and relationships. To be aware of any of them working in your life is a major first step in bringing pleasure back into your life and being accepting of romance entering your relationship. If you are not enjoying sex in your relationship or your orgasms are not intensely pleasurable, then guilt lurking somewhere in the background can be the reason. To be free of all guilt means you can be in a place to welcome romance and pleasure into your life without hesitation or inhibition. If you think guilt might be a problem for you, you might find a good therapist can completely revolutionise your relationships and thus your life.

If you are not enjoying sex in your relationship or your orgasms are not intensely pleasurable, then guilt lurking somewhere in the background can be the reason.

Guilt can be responsible for many different sexual disorders. But there are many other things responsible for trying to conspire against a woman which attempt to minimise her pleasure, arousal and responses. Notice the two following graphs and the role resistance plays in trying to mute sexual responsiveness.

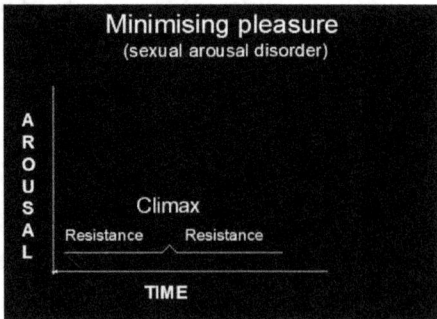

Figure 1

The first one reveals how arousal might be resisted by a woman's own body through being programmed by something such as guilt. Remember this would operate often at a subconscious level so that the woman would not even be aware of it driving the resistance. Regardless of how romantic her partner is or how romantic the setting is, there is a resistance that inhibits the natural sexual responses. The woman may just feel nothing. At worst she may feel annoyance at any sexual stimulation provided by her partner. There may be no vasodilation of the vulva and minimal or no lubrication response. But there is also minimal psychological involvement and connection. The woman is not *enjoying* the sexual encounter. The pleasure has been removed and the act degenerates into a chore. What results if lucky is an orgasm, but it is a resisted orgasm, one that becomes a mere bleep on the sexual screen. One that is easy to miss and leaves one wondering if that is all there is to it. Sex soon becomes a "take it or leave it" affair and when a busy life dictates that all unnecessary chores take a back seat, sex soon becomes way down the list of things to do.

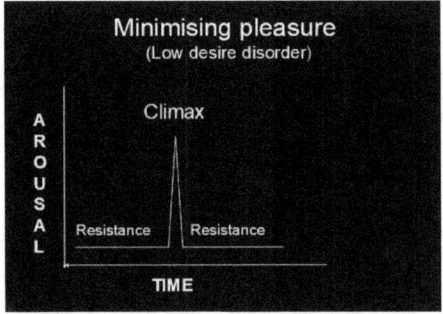

Figure 2

In the second graph you will notice that the climax is high in arousal and pleasure but it is still cut short in length and the build-up and afterglow is suppressed. The climax is still there but it is disconnected from the total experience. There is still resistance first up. Depending on the degree of resistance, sex may or may not get a chance to take place. It either becomes too hard or the initial desire is just not there to allow things to get started. One thing is very apparent. If there is little or no arousal or desire then romance, sexual pleasure and climax are just not going to get a chance to bloom.

HOW BIG THE PROBLEM REALLY IS

Low sexual desire is called Hypo Sexual Desire Disorder (HSDD) by sex therapists. And to be frank it is a way bigger problem than most people realise. While erectile dysfunction in men gets all the attention, medication and money thrown at it, HSDD in women is **THE** major problem for women. It is generally recognised by sexual therapists that HSDD is the number one issue for which women seek therapy. More than any other disorder, women seek out a sex therapist for low desire. Estimates are up to a third of the population may have HSDD. One can't wonder at how many people are suffering from HSDD in the general population and don't seek help for it or even realise that it is a disorder.

WHAT DEFINES IT?

How is HSDD defined and by whom? For instance is it defined by the person with the supposed HSDD or by their partner who is the one complaining about it? If it is the partner, then how does one know if he is just not suffering from Hyperactive Sexual Desire Disorder, or sexual addiction, and his partner's sex drive is actually normal? The subjectivity of the definition could produce a mine field of problems. The DSM-IV-TR defines HSDD by the following.

Criterion A

The essential feature of Hypoactive Sexual Desire Disorder is a deficiency or absence of sexual fantasies and desire for sexual activity.

Criterion B

The disturbance must cause marked distress or interpersonal difficulty.

Criterion C

The dysfunction is not better accounted for by another Axis I disorder (except another sexual dysfunction) and is not due exclusively to the direct physiological effects of a substance (including medications) or a general medical condition.

Low sexual desire may be global and encompass all forms of sexual expression or may be situational and limited to one partner or a specific sexual activity (eg. intercourse but not masturbation). There is little motivation to seek stimuli and diminished frustration when deprived of the opportunity for sexual expression. The individual usually does not initiate sexual activity or may only engage in it reluctantly when it is initiated by the partner. Although the frequency of sexual experiences is usually low, pressure from the partner or nonsexual needs (eg. for physical comfort or intimacy) may increase the frequency of sexual encounters... Apparent "low desire" in one partner may instead reflect an excessive need for sexual expression by the other partner. Alternatively, both partners may have levels of desire within the normal range but at different ends of the continuum."[14]

One of the interesting components is found in Criterion A which mentions a deficiency or absence of not only desire for sexual activity but also sexual fantasies. The point I take from this is that if you are not thinking about it, your desires are not going to be there either. It all starts in the mind. If you are not thinking about it, it is possible you have a disorder. Now we have all read how teenage boys are meant to be thinking about it on average every fourteen seconds throughout any given day! We also know testosterone is a big driver of sexual desire and men seem to have bucket loads for most of their lives. But women with healthy sex drives are also meant to be thinking about it. This is an interesting point about HSDD. A lot of women, and especially those in long term relationships, are just not thinking about sex throughout the day. Many don't fantasise about having sex with their partners that night. I know this because many women complain about sexual initiation by their partners as something that hits them out of the blue, without warning as if they just weren't expecting their partners would want sex with them tonight! For further information on this concept read the next chapter of romance under the sheets and think about how mind sex is so important to increase desire and pleasure but also how important mind sex is for women to prepare the brain and body for sex. The other part of the equation though is that although a lot of these women are not thinking about sex with their partners many of them I bet will be reading or would want to read romance novels and stories.

> *If you are not thinking about it, it is possible you have a disorder.*

INTERCOURSE ESTRANGEMENT

Often couples in their drive to get their needs met can set up counterproductive methods of reaching their goals. People of both genders can get stuck in roles of conflict and ways of expending energy that aren't working, but the person seems to think if he or she pushes harder, spends longer at it, that the desired result will eventually come. Therapists are meant to discover these ineffectual methods and provide insight to clients about how a change in behaviours can bring about lasting change, rather than a stubbornness to cling to old, fruitless patterns. This is why sexual therapy is often built on placing a ban on all sexual intercourse and getting the couple to reconnect with each other in a slow, non-threatening way through the use of sensate exercises. Old ineffectual and destructive patterns occur when men push women for sex which ends up becoming compulsive, loveless sex in a long term relationship. I have called it intercourse estrangement to provide the perspective from a woman's view.

Over years of a relationship, when the sexual activity is one-way, men work against their own goals which only cause resistance to sex in women. When loveless, compulsive sex characterises the sexual relationship of a couple, the woman starts to loathe sex. She might give in out of guilt or duty or power but when her heart is no longer in it, it quickly becomes a wedge that divides the couple. This will always lead to HSDD in women. Dr Rosie King (an Australian sex therapist) calls it "mercy sex". She says, "Guilt-motivated sex, or mercy sex, is pleasureless and does nothing for either party in the long run. Distancers who engage in mercy sex develop a strong sense of being used for sex. Distancer loss of self-esteem and feelings of worthlessness are the end result. Each time the distancer gives in to keep the peace... her desire will be turned down another notch."[15]

> *When loveless, compulsive sex characterises the sexual relationship of a couple, the woman starts to loathe sex.*

When such a cycle occurs, it can only be broken through taking the pressure off the pushing so that the resistance can stop. It is often men's comparatively high testosterone levels that push for **quantity** over **quality**. Men can easily confuse the two thinking quantity *is* quality. But nothing could be further from the truth. If quantity is quality, then men would settle for nothing but masturbation because of its accessibility. The truth is that men deeply crave for quality; their male ego derives a sense of worth from pleasing their partner sexually that virtually nothing else can do for them. Charlton in his book about treating sexual disorders alludes to this dilemma when he says, "Frequently the source of a desire discrepancy is not that the partners want contrasting amounts of sex but that they want contrasting types of sexual experiences – which they express as desiring contrasting amounts of sex."[16] So getting one partner to tolerate less sex while the other partner tries to tolerate more sex will just frustrate both partners.

The cycle can be broken when the pressure is taken off in terms of quantity while at the same time increasing the quality for both partners. It stands to reason that for many women with HSDD, they are simply just not enjoying sex that much. If it has no pleasure, and actually generates negative emotions or pain then women will have very little or no desire at all. Men need to understand this and a good therapist will be able to tactfully explain this to men. Once the quality and pleasure is increased for a woman, then desire can bloom.

THE TWO SWITCHES

What is actually happening when a woman does not feel aroused even when she might be trying hard to please her partner and even if physically she has signs of response such as vaginal lubrication? The term "frigid" was a terrible term probably once again invented by a man to describe a woman who could not be aroused. The issue is that any woman's body will respond to physical stimulation to a point, just the same as a man's body will respond to physical stimulation. In other words, physical stimulation produces a physiological response. In a woman this means things such as vaginal lubrication, hardening of the nipples and engorgement of the vulva. The problem though is that her mind is out of sync with her body's responses. Her thoughts, emotions and focus are not on the same journey as her initial bodily responses. Such a woman has in reality disconnected her mind from her body. A woman who lacks the associated feelings with the physical arousal her body might be producing has a major block which keeps the brain switch stuck on stop. So even though her body switch might be on "go", her brain switch is stuck on "stop". A woman needs **both** switches to be turned on in order for the process to work well. Often a woman in this situation leaves her brain switch set to stop but still goes through with the sexual encounter out of a sense of duty or to keep her partner happy or to stop herself from feeling guilty. Such a woman has not yet discovered the concept of the second switch, which is really the first switch, if she is going to maximise her pleasure of the sexual experience.

"So how is this switch set to go, you are probably asking?" "Quickly tell me before you ramble on about anything else." Okay then, here's the best piece of sexual advice a woman can ever get. The switch is simply an act of the will. The woman has to see herself as a sexual person. She has to program her mind to be a sexual person. She has to accept that she is a sexual being that allows herself to enjoy the giving and receiving of sexual pleasure. Her sexual identity has to be positive and rich in fully embracing her sexuality. Most of all, it has to be free of guilt because nothing gets the switch stuck on "stop" more than guilt.

When the brain switch is stuck on "stop", a woman's focus will be anywhere but on the sexual experience. Her mind will not be fantasising positive sexual experiences. Her mind will not be on enhancing her sexual pleasure. It will be distracted, it will be set on inhibiting desire rather than enhancing it. She will not be thinking or visualising during the day about letting go of everything later that night. Her brain switch will be stuck on "stop" all day every day and then when she is invited to participate in a sexual encounter by her partner she is then surprised as if it has hit her out of the blue! It surprises her way out of left field because her switch is still stuck on "stop". Then even when she is physically stimulated, her brain switch is still stuck on stop which will sabotage her sexual experience.

> *When the brain switch is stuck on "stop", a woman's focus will be anywhere but on the sexual experience.*

Both men and women are falsely told that women have to be turned on by a man. That "turn on" switch both men and women often think of in terms of physical attraction and stimulation. However, what we are not told is that there is a switch inside the woman's brain that can only be turned on by the woman **herself**. That switch is the one that the woman gives herself permission to go after sexual pleasure at that time. That switch is centred completely on her own pleasure. It has absolutely nothing to do with the responsibility to turn someone else on. It is purely focused on inviting, concentrating and enjoying the woman's own pleasure.

What happens though when a woman might try to turn the switch on but it seems stuck on stop no matter how much she wills it? This does happen to a lot of women. It especially happens to women who have had negative sexual experiences. Negative experiences to the extreme where rape or childhood abuse happens for instance can be paired with fear, anxiety and dread, or guilt (where the person might somehow blame themselves at least in part for the unpleasant experience) and can set like concrete in the early forming of a young woman's sexual identity. Whatever the negative experience, something has happened to block a woman for her to see herself positively in a sexual circumstance. Sometimes a young woman or girl can be abused and because of the physical stimulation her physical switch can get turned on. This means because of the physical stimulation she will have a physical response such as vaginal lubrication, even though this is against her will. This will be confusing for her because her mind switch is firmly switched to stop, yet her body will be signalling that it is turned on. Some women who have been through this experience will lay further false guilt on themselves. Some women even report experiencing orgasm during such abuse or rape even though their mind and voice might be screaming "stop!". To have traumatic experiences like these are a terrible scar left on one's sexual identity. The good news is that with the help of the right therapist, a woman can learn anew how to flick that brain switch on when she chooses, but also to enjoy what happens when the switch is turned to the "on" position. We don't have time to explore in depth the sexual therapy needed for women who have been deeply tortured by abuse but let's look at the basic concepts needed for a woman to reprogram her brain so she once again has the power to turn the brain switch to the "on" position.

Step one is to start visualising oneself as sexual. Start visualising oneself in erotic scenes and enjoying sexual intercourse. Imagine extreme pleasure from the sexual activity without even a hint of pain, ambivalence or awkwardness. All of the visualisation has to be positive, pleasurable and desired. If there have been previously negative mental images that have dominated the mind causing the switch to get stuck on "stop", then these must be replaced. The old ones must be let go of. They must be cremated rather than buried. By persistence the new ones can change the sexual identity into a positive one allowing the floodgates of pleasure to flow into one's life.

A word needs to be said here about acceptance. Whenever we have negative experiences in the past regardless of whether they are sexual or otherwise, we can often find ourselves engaged in a fight with them. We go over the mental images in our head, we try and change the scenario to turn out better, and we get stuck fighting them constantly. The trauma has a power over us because we keep fighting it. Instead of fighting the memories from the past which always has tentacles firmly wrapped around associated areas in our present reality, we need to learn the skill of acceptance. By learning the skill of acceptance means we understand and accept the reality of what happened. We never accept that it was right, or fair or meant to happen. We just accept that it did happen. Once we can embrace acceptance, all of a sudden those experiences start to lose their power and grip over us. It is as if our brain is telling us to look at the past experience because it is terrible, and it needs to get our attention. Our brain is screaming "What are you going to do about it?" So while ever we fight to repress it and bury it our brain is trying to push it back up to us again to have us deal with it. However, when acceptance comes, the brain doesn't have to keep pushing anymore. One can say, "Yes I know about that. It did happen, it wasn't fair, it shouldn't have happened but I know about it, I accept it as a reality in the past but I am now exercising my power in the present to build my present reality on my terms." The whole basis of mindfulness is centred around this concept. Accepting the past but being grounded and focused on the present so that feelings about the past or future don't have a chance to paralyse us with negative emotions.

Step two is to accept the physical stimulation and be actively focused on the pleasure associated with that stimulation and explore where it takes you. The trick is to **expect** that any sexual touching will be pleasurable and to anticipate its pleasure. Previously a woman may have been programmed to think of any sexual touching as unwanted, irritating or even painful. This reprogramming has to turn that around so that she expects and anticipates pleasure and is actively searching for it. By accomplishing these two steps a woman can then move from blocking the feelings associated with her physical responses and learn to enjoy the sexual caressing and foreplay.

Step three is to actively go after the pleasure. This leaves the switch firmly at the on position. This is the opposite to how sexual experiences might have been in the past when they were viewed as a chore, boring or lacking all pleasure. Sometimes some women are too self-conscious about the bodily responses of sexual pleasure and climax. For instance such things as deeper breathing, breath holding, moans and groans, feet extending and facial grimacing are often incorrectly taken as negative responses. When they are viewed as negative they are then inhibited. But they are all part of the sexual excitement and pleasure process. These have to be viewed as positive. Some sexual therapists get women to practise all these responses so that they are not foreign during sex. Sometimes women are encouraged to exaggerate these responses during sex. Amazingly these can actually heighten the sexual experience and the associated pleasure because it kicks the brain switch so firmly to the "on" position that it breaks off and gets stuck at the "on" position clearing the sexual experience of all inhibitions and blocks. Let's have a look now at how this works physiologically.

> **It kicks the brain switch so firmly to the "on" position that it breaks off and gets stuck at the "on" position...**

THE SCIENCE BEHIND AROUSAL

There are two opposite states which both play a part in the sexual experience. Look back several pages to figures 1 and 2 titled minimising pleasure. You will notice that there is resistance first of all which inhibits pleasure, arousal and climax. This state could also be thought of as an anxiety state. Whether it is a distracted state, or whether it is a frustrated state of wanting to get things over and done with (mercy sex), or whether it is a state of anxiety about what the partner is thinking and whether the woman is ticking all the boxes and pleasing her partner (spectator sex – we will talk more about this later), they are all states which cause a stress response. This stress response is a state which excites the sympathetic nervous system to respond in either fight, flight or freeze. It is a state of hyper-vigilance for the brain. It means the connections in the woman's brain are quicker and sharper so that connections are made so quickly that it seems like thoughts speed in at the speed of light but can just as quickly leave as something else takes their place. The problem is that these rapid thoughts all steal pleasure form the woman. It ensures the brain switch remains firmly in the "stop" position. But it also does something else. It actually minimises the arousal mechanisms that are meant to flow freely from a relaxed state. The parasympathetic nervous system regulates these involuntary responses. These responses include blood flow to the genital areas that enhance sensations, the vaginal lubrication that allows penetration and can remove the possibility of pain, the relaxing of the vaginal control muscles which also release the tension, tightness and barriers to the smooth entering of the penis, and the calm state of safety needed to relax and accept the pleasure.

So the process has actually been reversed so that the anxiety state minimises the responses very early, inhibits the pleasure, distracts the brain, increases the likelihood of pain and keeps that brain switch welded to the "stop" position. The fascinating part of the process though is that there is a change that takes place to allow climax, if and when it happens. In the lead up there has been physical stimulation and there might have been some pleasure trying to get in around the resistance, distraction and inhibition. If the woman gives in to the climax and allows it to happen, it happens under pressure and there is a quick acceptance to almost begrudgingly allow the climax to take place. Remember that up until now there has been some active pressure against climax from happening, through all the distraction, resistance, inhibiting and the disconnection of the brain from the physiological pleasurable responses. But this relaxing, which is more a giving in under pressure and resistance, is only allowed for a second or two to allow climax and then control is taken back to resist again. You might have noticed by now that this whole process is the very opposite of what very pleasurable sex looks like. So instead of resistance, then letting go to quickly climax and then taking back over to resist again, let's see what the exact opposite of this process might look like.

What we want from the very beginning is a very relaxed state rather than the stress response. We want a woman to be accepting rather than resisting at the very beginning. That relaxed state provided by the parasympathetic nervous system does a number of things. Firstly, it communicates the message that it is safe to flick the brain switch to on. Secondly, it allows the woman to look for the arousal responses, to focus on finding them through expecting them and inviting them. Thirdly, it presents a relaxed state which allow and encourage those arousal responses to happen. These are the vaginal lubrication, the relaxed muscle tone, the hardening of the nipples and the release of the connecting oxytocin hormone. There is continuing interest and study in the hormone oxytocin. It is often called the "cuddle hormone" and is known for its maternal and bonding effects. Further areas of study are now investigating its role in increasing orgasm, decreasing anxiety and cortisol levels (we will talk about cortisol later) and the bonding effect it exerts such as between mother and child. Fourthly, the relaxed state allows the flow and acceptance of pleasurable sensations.

Having a stress free zone in the early phase of arousal sedates the brain connections so that single focus is easier. Stress can make the brain connections quicker and allows too many other connections to take centre stage. This relaxed state is often sought by lovers through the use of wine before lovemaking. When the relaxed state is achieved it allows the pleasurable sensations to be exactly that, pleasurable. Hyper vigilance is let go of so that concentration can explore the pleasure from arousal.

However, if this passive, relaxed state driven by the parasympathetic nervous system is allowed to continue to dominate then the climax will still be muted. Once the early parasympathetic arousal responses have done their job, an awakening of desire takes hold. This change means that desire has taken hold of the reigns and that desire wants more. More pleasure, more bonding, more responses and more enjoyment. This means a change from a passive condition to an active one. You might think that changing from a relaxed state to a stress response, or sympathetic one would kill everything and minimise the pleasure. But here is the amazing thing because it actually enhances it. The enhancing comes because under the right conditions there is a flip side to the sympathetic nervous system. It not only displays itself in stress responses of fight, flight and freeze. This other side is revealed in athletes just before they compete at the very top level. Instead of becoming completely frozen in front of the crowd they use it to become **excited**. A boy playing on his skate board suddenly notices a girl he likes is watching him. Straightaway his performance increases and he starts to become daring in his jumps and tricks as he wants to show off. This is because the very same responses of the sympathetic nervous system, or stress responses are the same as being excited. The heart beat quickens, the breathing rate increases, the palms may become sticky, and the brain connections improve. The best athletes know how to control these stress responses and use them to their advantage. They are the ones who love the big stage and perform on it with complete enjoyment. They become addicted to it. They come to love it. Another example would be a public speaker or musician who loves presenting or singing to huge crowds. So many people would be terrified if they had to present or sing in front of thousands of people but others get excited by it. They actively choose to put themselves in that situation which to another would have caused terror.

So the opening up to the pleasurable responses increases desire, increases pleasure and increases **excitement**. The active response is where the woman becomes excited and now goes after sexual pleasure. The most amazing fact is that a woman can either inhibit or enhance her orgasms. We have talked a lot about how a woman might inhibit her responses and orgasms. However, by a woman connecting with her physical, sexual responses, flicking the brain switch by saying, "yes please" and then actively pursuing genital stimulation and everything that might go with lovemaking, the longer and more intense the orgasms can become. The more the active seeking after the pleasure, the more the body is encouraged to respond orgasmically.

> ***The most amazing fact is that a woman can either inhibit or enhance her orgasms.***

Something needs to be made clear here. The woman needs to be in control of her sexuality and her decision. When the woman gives her control up to her partner she loses her responsibility. Many women have the misconception that it should be their partner's responsibility to turn them on. Nothing could be further from the truth. When a woman expects her man to be responsible for her sexual pleasure she has returned to the passive state and robs herself of the potential intensity and extended time of her orgasms. In contrast, when a woman takes responsibility for her own sexual pleasure, she is becoming active in the process, she is flicking the inner brain switch herself to the "go" position and she has become more attuned to the pleasure that results. She can actually *feel* the pleasure more intensely. She is doing more than welcoming it at the front door. She has gone out the front door and has actively gone searching for it to grab it with both hands and squeeze every bit of pleasure out of it. By actively seeking out the pleasure in the sexual experience, the woman switches from seeking to please her partner to taking responsibility for her own sexual pleasure. The amazing side effect though is that this actually pleases her partner like nothing else does.

So what happens after the climax? In our model of low arousal you will notice there was resistance actively returning quickly after any climax. In the opposite model however, when a woman takes responsibility to firstly relax, accept the arousal responses and invite the pleasuring, and then willingly flick the internal brain switch to "go" so that the passive relaxed state becomes an active state full of desire seeking climax and stimulation, then after climax the woman can return to the passive, relaxed, parasympathetic state which allows her to marinate in the afterglow experience. This means that once the desire has been fulfilled and the excitement of the sympathetic system has completed its mission, the body and mind can relax and slump into the soaking up of the pleasure. With such an opposite model of sexuality, the model full of desire and increased pleasure looks something like this.

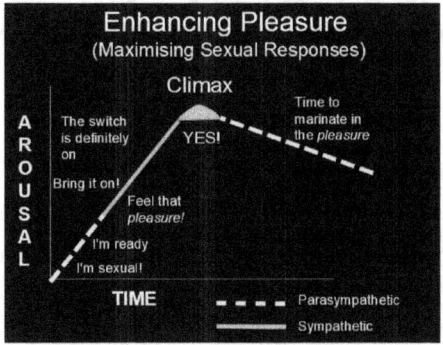

Figure 3

MENOPAUSE – THROWING THE SPANNER IN THE WORKS

The simple fact is that women are living longer. But this longevity has revealed an extra challenge for women. Women now live a third of their lives or longer in a post-menopausal state. So what do we know about the affect menopause has on women's sexuality? Unfortunately it's not good news. Sexual dysfunction increases dramatically after the time of menopause. Professor Dennerstein's work in Australia showed that 88%, nearly nine out of ten women, seven years after the onset of menopause have one or more kinds of sexual dysfunction. Furthermore, 81.2% were distressed about this change. Of course once again, the main areas of sexual dysfunction found were a decrease in sexual desire and sexual responsiveness (including sexual arousal, enjoyment and orgasm), and a decrease in frequency of sexual activities.[17]

This is a shocking finding. But it gets even worse when we consider the amount of women who have hysterectomies before they would naturally transition to a menopausal state. These are women who have their uterus removed for various medical reasons. Some even have to have their ovaries surgically removed which further complicates matters and have a further profound effect on sexual functioning. These women will lose even more oestrogen as well as lose about half the level of testosterone they would have without the full surgery. Hysterectomy is also not an exact science when it comes to nerve sparing which means that there is the possibility of sexual nerves being cut during surgery.

CHEMICAL ANSWERS

Once menopause takes place either naturally or surgically, there is a decline in the hormones oestrogen, progesterone and testosterone. Reduced testosterone levels lead to a sudden or gradual loss in sex drive. Ironically, the conventional hormone replacement therapy of oestrogen and progesterone given to relieve menopausal symptoms can make matters worse, because oestrogen increases a protein (called steroid hormone-binding globulin) in the blood that binds to testosterone, causing it to become less available in the body. This means there is a case for women already on hormone replacement therapy (HRT) who have hypoactive sexual desire disorder (HSDD) to consider having testosterone added, provided there are no other causes for the HSDD.

Testosterone is **the** hormone which produces sex drive in both genders. Women have far lower levels, but they are also far more sensitive to it. The correct blood serum levels of testosterone for women should be a minimum of 1.9 for free testosterone and a minimum of 20 of total testosterone. A simple blood test can confirm what the levels are. The problem is, women's testosterone levels gradually decrease with age which can result in HSDD. One of the major problems is maintaining the correct level for therapeutic effect, especially when women self-medicate. This happens for example when women purchase a 2% testosterone cream over the internet and apply it without medical monitoring. Doctors have reported testosterone levels ten times over the normal limit in such cases. This can be a serious issue as even women taking the correct dose and who are monitored can report side effects including lower levels of high density lipoprotein (this is the good cholesterol you need to lower cardiovascular disease risk abbreviated to HDL), acne, hirsutism (abnormal growth of hair on a woman's face and body), clitoromegaly (your clitoris growing huge – wait is that a bad thing my male brain is screaming? At least a man would have no excuse if he couldn't find it!) and voice deepening.

Testosterone is THE hormone which produces sex drive in both genders.

So there are risks as there are with taking any medications. But there does seem a role for testosterone therapy in selected women who have no other causes for HSDD. However, co-administration with oestrogen therapy should be provided to prevent unwanted effects of high density lipoprotein levels and patients should be made aware of the risks. Furthermore, women with current or previous breast cancer, uncontrolled hyperlipidemia, liver disease, acne or hirsutism should not receive testosterone therapy.[18] In general oestrogen increases vaginal lubrication and strengthens vaginal walls and deal with sexual dysfunctions related to dyspareunia (painful intercourse) whereas testosterone deals with sex drive.

Flibanserin is a new medication for HSDD. It is a multi-functional serotonin agonist and antagonist which means it acts to both suppress and encourage certain properties of serotonin. It results in an increase in dopamine and norepinephrine activity. Dopamine affects desire and arousal and may promote willingness to continue sexual activity after it is initiated, so an increase in dopamine activity is a positive thing. In the USA, Flibanserin is so far the only drug approved by the FDA for treating HSDD in premenopausal women. In trials it worked equally well in post-menopausal women but it has not been approved for such women at the time of writing. Women who take the non-hormonal medication need to take the daily dosing of 100mg at bedtime to minimise any possible side effects. It can take several weeks to feel any results so women who have been prescribed the drug are encouraged to try it for a couple of months before giving up on it if it doesn't produce the desired results.

The future of drug therapy for treatment of HSDD will continue to evolve as new treatment options become available and research in this area grows. The drug bremelanotide is still being trialled at the time of publishing however, it has demonstrated clinical efficacy in phase 2 studies.[19] Whether chemical treatments alone, a psychological approach or a combination of the two is the best approach will vary from person to person. The interaction between various drugs and the effect that psychological interventions have on chemical balances and imbalances remains unclear. However, when it comes to chemical influences it seems that HSDD is attributed to either an imbalance in sexual excitatory pathways (dopamine, norepinephrine, melanocortin and oxytocin) or sexual inhibitory pathways (serotonin, opioid, endocannabinoid and prolactin) or a combination of both.[20]

So the good news is that there is help in our modern age whether it be medication, psychotherapy or a combination of the two. When it comes to menopause there are some positives that researchers have discovered. The first one is the level of sexual functioning a woman has before she enters menopause (so if you are happy sexually entering menopause, this will exert a positive effect on menopausal and post-menopausal sexual functioning). A second factor is that if a woman gains a new partner during or after menopause then this can have a very positive influence on her sexual functioning. Finally, a woman's positive feelings for her partner are also a positive influence on her sexual functioning.[21] These three areas are a key I believe to the important role romance plays in healthy, positive, sexual functioning in any woman whether it be a premenopausal, menopausal or post-menopausal period. All three of these factors would describe a woman who is strongly, **romantically** connected to her partner. Romance is a key ingredient at any time in a woman's life if she wants to experience the potential of her intimate relationship.

SUMMARY OF CHAPTER SEVEN

Early religious teaching was that sexual pleasure was sin.
This was a very different teaching to the Bible which promotes a more healthy view of sexuality.
These dark ages' views still influence women today.
Women can easily catch this false guilt which will inhibit their sexuality, desire and pleasure.
Guilt and other things create strong resistance to arousal and pleasure in women.
Hypo Sexual Desire Disorder (HSDD) is a huge problem that effects many women.
Intercourse estrangement develops from "mercy sex".
A woman and her partner need to understand the **two** switches.
Negative sexual experiences can get the internal brain switch stuck on "stop".
3 steps to removing it from the stuck on "stop" position include:
i) Visualising oneself as sexual
ii) Actively focusing on physical stimulation and expecting it to be pleasurable
iii) Actively going after the pleasure
Some sexual disorders are characterised by sympathetic nervous system control (active resistance) followed by parasympathetic nervous system control (letting go) momentarily, followed by sympathetic control again (active resistance).
But this process should be reversed to gain maximal pleasure.
To do this the sympathetic nervous system becomes excited rather

than resistant.

Menopause can exert a negative influence on sexual functioning. Chemical answers include testosterone, Flibanserin and possibly soon Bremelanotide.

A woman who is strongly romantically connected to her partner has a protective factor to sexual disorders through and post menopause.

8

CHAPTER EIGHT

ROMANCE UNDER THE SHEETS

"You always have time for romance, even if you don't always have time for sex".
(Paul Gaughan)

There are two types of sex for women, often described as great sex and not so great sex, but what makes sex great, and what makes it a chore? Romance is what can make the difference. Romance is usually one of the main ingredients of the best sex for women. While it is generally true that most men want more sex while most women want more love, it is when men begin to give more love and romance that women can want more sex and it becomes more enjoyable for them. So the fundamental question is, how can more love and romance be injected into your relationship **under** the sheets? This chapter will explore a variety of answers to this question.

We can often understand how the very first sexual experience with someone we are attracted to, can be romantic and exciting if only for the sake of its newness. But how can making love to the same partner for years be just as romantic? Let's analyse some common threads that run through new relationships and see how we can adapt them to fit into not so new ones. As you read through the various points see how they are related to your own courtship and ponder how these ingredients can be blended back into your own relationship today.

> *It is when men begin to give more love and romance that women can want more sex and it becomes more enjoyable for them.*

A. BACK AT THE BEGINNING
1. Life Was Simple.

Generally speaking, when we are younger we are more carefree. The older we get we become more staid in our ways and more resistant to change. As our relationship grows so do our age and our dependence upon the routines and systems we have learned to feel secure in. Not only is our ability to handle change easier in our twenties, but we didn't seem to have the complex problems that we have now. True, we usually make the biggest decisions in life when we are younger - whom we will marry, what career we will choose, what house we will buy, and how many children we will have. But it isn't till after courtship and the early years of our relationship that we become trapped and engrossed in the details of those decisions. This is when you are actually living with your mate with all of his now glaring faults, juggling career roles with home roles and the demands from both; stretching the budget to pay for the mortgage, and feeding, clothing, keeping healthy, educating and being totally responsible for the little darlings. Add to that the extra pressures of stress, fatigue, in-laws and the sensitive balance to maintain necessary and desired interpersonal relationships and you will agree life has definitely become more complex.

So is it possible to change our complex lives or are we destined to be suffocated in the tangled web of our own making? It is true that there are some things we cannot change. The mortgage repayments still have to be met and we just can't opt out of society to get back to basics. But here are a few suggestions to help.

a) Change the things you can. You can't change everything but that doesn't mean you can't change some things. Assess those areas in your week that you can change and ask yourself whether you are really happy doing what you are doing with that time. Are you too busy with things that matter least? Does that committee really need you? Or more to the point, do you really need that committee? You may need to draw on those reservoirs of assertiveness you have somewhere deep down inside (can you find them?), in order to make those necessary adjustments. Are you too busy, period? Slow down, the world will not fall apart if you let go of a few unnecessary items.

b) Keep your life in balance. If a spin-drier on a washing machine loses balance you know the result. The faster it works the more out of balance it seems. So it is with a busy life. Keep balance in your own life by allowing yourself time out and activities that will increase your ability to cope rather than drain you of your reserves of emotional and physical energy.

Take up a hobby, play a sport or set aside a time at least once a week to do something you really enjoy doing. Better still if your mate really enjoys it too and you can do it together. Make sure you have attainable goals, both short and long term and that you can also spend some time each week working towards those goals.

c) Reduce killers and increase the aphrodisiacs. It stands to reason that the more negatives you remove from your life and the more positives you add, are all going to combine to make your life far more positive. By adding romance to your program, pampering yourself with a few luxuries now and again and indulging yourself with an occasional decadent treat, you are making yourself a more relaxed, happier partner for your mate to love. Increase the pleasantries and all things that make you feel sexy, alive and more desirous for your spouse. Make time for those long bubble baths before you go to bed.

d) Keep healthy. Remember that a healthy body makes a healthy mind and visa versa. If you are fit and well you can normally cope with the everyday stresses we all have to endure. An investment in the good health of your body is the best investment you will ever make. Remind yourself frequently of the nutritional basics, which are not only important for yourself but also for your whole family, especially if you find yourself responsible for their meals as well. Large quantities of carbohydrates and sugars (junk food) feed depression and sluggishness. Make these foods treats rather than a staple diet. Concentrate on fresh fruit and vegetables, and let your body show you how good you should feel all the time. A regular exercise program can never be underestimated. The natural high you can receive from endorphins released when you exercise can not only help you feel good about yourself but also make you prepared for the onslaughts of a demanding lifestyle.

e) Learn to relax. Sleep deprivation can have drastic effects upon anyone. If you are so stressed out from the demands of the day that you cannot relax to go to sleep, you need help. Insomnia can be dealt with in natural ways rather than treating the symptoms by dosing oneself with sleeping tablets. These natural ways include stress management classes, learning relaxation techniques, meditation, investing in a comfortable bed, exercise, proper diet with regular meals, going to bed at the same time every night, learning to wind down before bedtime (by participating in relaxing activities such as longer baths, relaxing music and soothing recreational pursuits like reading) and making sure that you don't take your problems to bed with you so that your conscious mind doesn't continually race when it's meant to be stopped. Banning all screen time at least a couple of hours before bed can also help as the light from electronic screens tricks the brain into believing it is daytime.

Furthermore, if you can learn the art of relaxing for a minute or two every hour, or at least sprinkled throughout the day, you can increase productivity and relieve small stresses before they can accumulate into draining proportions. Tiredness can kill any aphrodisiac and override any amorous or romantic feelings. By getting a good night's sleep you not only rally your forces for the onslaught of the new day, but you make sure you are more open to romance either when you wake up, during the day or under the sheets the next night.

Tiredness can kill any aphrodisiac and override any amorous or romantic feelings.

f) Attitude. Your attitude can determine whether you survive or die with some of life's twists. The direction you face your mind can make all the difference. Acceptance is a wonderful asset when you know you have done your best to change something. Brooding over tragedies or problems for long periods just creates deeper problems. But for those things that can be changed or should be changed, adopt a positive attitude. Don't procrastinate on problem areas in your life that need changing. Work out a plan, a strategy to deal with it and then a time frame of when it will take place. Even by the very act of addressing problem areas by actually working out a strategy to solve them, you can disarm the fear involved.

Basically you can choose to be happy, sad, depressed, angry or any of the emotions. Don't let problems govern your attitude - let your attitude govern your problems. There will always be something in your life you can allow yourself to become depressed over. Choose each day to be contented and happy, there will always be another day to be depressed. Happiness is not a matter of external happenings; it is rather a state of being, an attitude. Choose it, develop it, strengthen it and refuse to give it up and watch your life grow as a result. So often we over-invest ourselves into things that matter very little. Whether it be someone else's drama, wanting to be right, looking good at all costs or picking fights we can never win. Think about the negative issues that come our way all the time. If you react to every one of them with all your fierceness, where will you end up? Probably a nervous wreck. Many people do, because they can't make the distinction between what really matters and what doesn't. You and I have met people who are highly reactive. Everything is so black and white. They will even lecture you on how to tie your shoe laces the correct way and woe to you if you don't follow their exact advice for the rest of your life! Let it go. Let go of everything that doesn't matter, and you will with wisdom discover that happens to be the vast majority of everything. Social media has spawned a whole generation which is obsessed with how many likes they can get. But how much is enough? Self-esteem, body image, how I feel and my whole mental health is now being determined by everyone else including the online trolls. Take back your life. Invest in what is really important in your life and experience the liberation. Stop reacting to everyone and everything. Instead choose to respond to what you truly want to invest your self into. Observe life, you don't have to absorb everything.

Don't let problems govern your attitude - let your attitude govern your problems.

g) Recognise the bad times. Choosing a positive attitude to life doesn't mean that you always will be free from depression or negative feelings. What it does mean is that you are facing a positive direction. There may be times of disappointment but it is not going to change your direction in life. What you should do, if you suffer from depression of some type, is to acknowledge it to yourself when it happens, so you can make the necessary adjustments as required. By acknowledging it, you can deal with it more positively and look to it more as a valley on the happiness road rather than a change in direction. Furthermore, by recognising a mood swing, you know that you are not necessarily to blame for how you feel, rather it is just a part of life that needs to be accepted for what it is. The good part is knowing that it is only transitory, it won't last, it's only a natural hiccup. Ease your workload during this time, pay special attention to nutrition, do your best to get the right amount of uninterrupted sleep and try getting your mind off yourself by doing something nice for someone else.

h) No unnatural crutches. Sometimes the call of an unnatural escapism can be alluring especially if our lives are complex or fast. Don't allow yourself to be fooled into the misconception that drugs can prop you up, steady your nerves or provide a necessary escapism. They can only offer a pseudo, temporary relief of the symptoms, while they lead you away from dealing with the cause. A dependence upon drugs can lead to greater problems and mask your body's warning signals.

If you could remove modern, western complexities from your life and just escape to a tropical island inhabited only by you and your man, then you would probably find your man a lot more romantic, in such a romantic environment. Anyone could be, at least for a while anyway. But even though buying a tropical island is impossible for most of us, we can still avoid some of the complex, stressful routines we commit ourselves to. We may be able to afford a tropical island holiday for a few weeks of the year and regain our lives, which were simpler when we first met our lover. We may even be able to inject some island life back home by learning the fun of breaking routines and getting back to basics, the things that really count in our lives like relationships to loved ones.

2. We Used To Have Limitless Energy When We Fell In Love.
Something that characterises when we first fall in love more than anything else is that we have more energy. There is something about being

in love that puts zest into everything we do and life in general takes on a more positive appearance.

Do you remember how late you used to stay out of a night and yet still managed to get up for work the next day? Could you live life now at such a hectic pace? Many people say that it is age that makes the difference. Back then you were young and could keep up with the fast lane. But age is not the determining factor, romantic love is. I have a friend in his eighties who has just met the woman of his dreams (who is incidentally older than he is) and would you believe that come 9:00 PM he is not tucked away in bed any more but together they are out dancing the night away. Yes, regardless of age, people seem to double their energy levels when romance rules their lives.

Age is not the determining factor, romantic love is.

It seems that part of the apathy that results from the ageing of a relationship makes an attitude of "I can't be bothered making the effort." "Who notices", or "who wants to join my efforts?" is also a concern aimed at one's spouse. But someone somehow has to break the cycle of a lifeless relationship and if it's not your partner then it has to be you. It is worth making the effort, life can be fun and the future can hold so much fun, adventure and romance for you and your partner together. The secret is firstly to ***plan*** to have energy. Look for those areas in your timetables that are the slack ones and when there is less chance of tiredness from the night before. When you plan for a special romantic time, make sure you both go to bed early the night before, so you can draw on those extra reserves of energy.

Secondly, push yourself a little. We extend our energy levels for all sorts of reasons - the children, work, other people, relatives, finances and projects so why not romance? Make the effort if you think effort is what it will take. You deserve it, your relationship needs it and your whole world will be better off because of it. It is a lot like trying to make yourself happy. If you make sure you smile a lot even if you don't feel happy, then after a while your smiling can affect your attitude. If you keep making yourself smile then after a while you don't have to force yourself - it starts to come naturally. So too with energy and romance, after you push yourself a little and enjoy the romance, you start to find it easier and easier until it doesn't become an effort but a desire like it did in the earlier days. Another spin off is that you not only have more energy for romance outside the bedroom, you both have more energy under the sheets as well.

3. It Used To Be Priority Number One
Closely linked to our energy level was the fact that we reserved our energy for our most important priority - our romantic relationship. Somewhere between then and now, however, our romantic priorities have been pushed down the list. Back then the relationship was the all-consuming power in our lives, and priorities were clearly defined. But with added responsibilities it is the relationship that seems to be always put on hold. There is no magical recipe to get your relationship back to number one priority other than just making a conscious decision to put it there and learning to stick by it. Our priorities are made by us and we have the final say as to what will and will not rule our lives. We need to use our power of choice and endeavour to remind ourselves of that choice.

What is frustrating is how the amount of non-consequential things can rob us of our time, which should be channelled into our high priorities. Have you ever noticed that the things that take so much of our time are often the least important? Big businesses realise the importance of time management and are not afraid to spend huge amounts of money on their employees in seminars and the like to learn the principles of "prioritising" and time management. They see it as an investment to get the most out of their employees. You too can learn the principles of "prioritising" and time management that top managers use to blend into your own circumstances, so that you can save time for romantic priorities. There are seminars, plenty of books available and lots of free information online for you if you think you can benefit in this area. It can be amazing if you just gather together those single minutes of time that we let escape each day. If we find a useful purpose for these we may benefit for hours during the course of a week. That time alone saved and substituted could be the answer to our romantic dreams. Furthermore, if we can reduce the amount of repetition in our routines, we may have the time to add new things to our relationship so that our romantic priorities can be realised.

Make a time with your man when both of you can list the top five priorities in your life and alongside them list the amount of time each week these items receive. When finished swap lists and discuss the variables and where there are other lower priorities that get more time assigned to them and why. Make it a time of insight and growth rather than for an attack upon the other. Then together make a list of priorities from the two lists and allot the time you would realistically see devoted to each one. By making sure romance figures on your mutual list you may in this way ensure a commitment from your spouse to romance. Sometimes our priorities can become too undefined, too unclear for us to understand and we are left to every whim and force that may pull at us for attention, to define our priorities for us. By a simple exercise in listing our priorities, we define them clearly and suggest the time each deserves. By putting them on paper we highlight, expose and remind one another of the importance of individual priorities including romance and love.

> *Sometimes our priorities can become too undefined, too unclear for us to understand and we are left to every whim and force that may pull at us for attention, to define our priorities for us.*

4. Both Partners Used To Look Their Best

Do you remember when you first met your mate how you took extra care over your appearance? You may not have dared to let your future spouse see you without your hair done or without you looking your best. He was probably just the same. But now your long term relationship allows you to see your spouse in the most unflattering of positions and times. In addition, age, child bearing and workloads all work their hardest to carve away at your figure to leave you feeling far from your most entrancing.

It's not practical to have your make-up on twenty-four hours a day. But you should be aware that men are most attuned to visual stimuli. It is what they see that turns them on. Don't be paranoid about your appearance but keep it in mind and use it to your advantage at appropriate times such as before bedtime. Something we tend to overlook is that we probably presented the best of our personality and ourselves to our partner when we first met them. A happy, sexy personality can stimulate many a man to unveil his romantic identity and encourage him to take the effort to look his best as well.

5. Sharing, Connecting And Learning About The Other Used To Prelude Lovemaking.

In my book, *How To Dramatically Increase Your Wife's Sex Drive*, in the chapter dedicated to romance I mentioned "romantic triggers."[22] These are things that help create a romantic environment and make it easy to be romantic. Things like music, discovery of new knowledge and natural beauty can be romantic triggers. When we are first in love with our partner there is often a high frequency of these romantic triggers in our lives. As we went out together on dates we grew in understanding and appreciation of the other and our relationship grew too. But when did you learn the last, new exciting thing about your man? Can you remember? No doubt if we kept up the high frequency of romantic stimulants and the sharing and connecting with our partner then the romance also would have continued. Those deep times of talking about our feelings, our dreams, our fears and just intimately "knowing" the other can never be underestimated for their growth building and romantic injection into our relationship. It is true that we don't really know a person until we have exposed and shared our innermost thoughts and feelings to them, taken the risk of trusting them, laughed and cried with them. Make room in your relationship for connecting together, whether it be driving in the car, going for a walk or in bed before you go to sleep and watch the pathway to romance widen and become stronger.

> *If we kept up the high frequency of romantic stimulants and the sharing and connecting with our partner then the romance also would have continued.*

6. Love Used To Be Blind

One fascinating aspect about falling in love is its emphasis on playing down the negatives and concentrating on the positives in the beloved one. Love is blind to the faults of the other, giving him or her a fantasy image that he or she is expected to carry with them for the rest of their lives. It is perhaps this aspect of fantasy that can be romanticised and even divorced from the people themselves when they don't seem to be living up to the image originally created. But living in a fantasy world is not true romance because sooner or later one is brought back to reality, and the further away one has been, the greater the thud on return. True romance is accepting the other person with all their faults, loving them unconditionally, but still managing to concentrate on the positives in a relationship. Many unromantic couples only ever seem to let the points of contention dominate their relationship. When this happens the balance has to be reversed so that the negatives are lost sight of because of the pleasure of voluntary exposure and absorption of the positives in the relationship. So practically, in your relationship with your man, you must learn to concentrate on the positives you both have while at the same time resolve any negatives you have. Unfortunately many people cannot do this and the romantic atmosphere of the relationship disappears.

Negative issues in relationships are dealt with through communication and a strong commitment from both sides to the good of the relationship. Sometimes negative issues that are fought over are not resolved straight away. At other times they are only resolved for one party. To preserve romance in your relationship you must learn not only to resolve negatives but learn to not take them to bed. In fact, if a couple could learn to never take any negatives to bed, negatives from their relationship, work or life in general, then just imagine the barriers to romance in the bedroom that would be removed.

Many unromantic couples only ever seem to let the points of contention dominate their relationship.

7. Mind Sex

It takes a conscious decision of commitment to not allow yourself to dwell on all of the negatives when you go to bed. Young lovers who don't have any barriers to lovemaking and who find the earth really moves for them in earthquake proportions, are people who dwell on positives when they look for romance under the sheets. Make it a rule to commit yourself to overwhelming your mind with positive thoughts when you get into bed. Practise putting your partner in romantic, luxurious settings with power at his fingertips and people, especially women, everywhere admiring him and wanting to be noticed by him. But it is you that turns his eye, it is you that he desires, it is you that he goes after. Thinking positive thoughts is such a simple task once it is practised and mastered. It is good therapy for depression, stress and insomnia as well as your sex life. Try it, get rid of those negative thoughts and see how it prepares you for romance under the sheets like nothing else!

This is something that is possible for you to control completely by yourself, but it can also be enhanced and developed by your lover. In my book, *How To Dramatically Increase Your Wife's Sex Drive*, I explained to men the importance, and the how to, of making love to a woman's mind. There is a real art that a man can develop with a little practice. Unfortunately, this art seems to be lost soon after a relationship develops and matures, that is, if the man knew the art to begin with. In this age of short cuts, time saving and fast food, isn't it a tragedy that making love to a woman's mind gets left out so repeatedly. Because a woman's mind is not a physical, visually recognised thing on the outside of her body, a man has trouble seeing it. If he could see it in relation to its importance, a woman's sexual being would be largely made up of her mind. The secret a lot of men do not realise is that a woman's mind is her biggest sexual organ - yet it is the one that gets left out of lovemaking the most.

The process used to be make love to a woman's mind first and this step would prepare her body. Today, however, many couples short circuit the whole process of lovemaking by leaving step one out altogether. Many men have lost the art of making love to a woman's mind and believe that a tube of lubrication brings the same results. It may give physical similarities but a woman knows that making love goes beyond the physical and begins with your mind. Help your man understand the importance of making love to your mind first and to enjoy the natural cascades of making love without using lubrication every time from a tube.

> *Today many couples short circuit the whole process of lovemaking by leaving step one out altogether.*

One unique way of helping men explore this concept is to encourage them to include the narration of a romantic story now and again as a special form of foreplay. With a little creativity a man can create and tell his partner romantic stories as he gently caresses her body and places both partners in romantic settings. This can be a dramatic form of foreplay where a few factors combine together to produce romantic dynamite.

First of all there is the fantasy factor. You can travel the world and have any lifestyle with power and money having no limit. It is a more powerful fantasy because it is not originating in your mind but in your lover's. This introduces mystery and anticipation as the story unfolds, and makes it more powerful as it comes from the voice of your mate. Your partner is not limited to any budget for roses, banquets or gifts.

In addition, this foreplay time involves your man talking to you and communicating by touch. Just the very fact of hearing your man speaking romantic, sexy themes to you can be deeply satisfying and a real key to turning you on. Women often complain of the absence of their partner's voice in lovemaking, especially in the foreplay stage, but story telling can change this completely. It can also help your man to express and verbalise his feelings to you using this play acting medium, which can be a lot less threatening for a man. It can also help bridge the gap between him thinking the thoughts and expressing them to you at other times.

Furthermore, the touching, caressing, stroking and fondling all make the story more real as the partner incorporates the actual acts into the story line. He plays out the story line by touching you all over your body. Here are a few pointers for your lover to keep in mind when he tells you the romantic, adult bedtime story.

1. You must have your eyes shut.
2. You can start with your clothes on or off, in bed or in another room but you must keep your eyes shut the whole time in order to preserve the illusion. A blindfold may even be appropriate!
3. The story must start off slow and not go straight to sex.

4. It is good for the hero to tease and build desire and possibly even have a short lull in his advances in order to drag out foreplay.
5. It is important for the storyteller (the man) to tell his partner the feelings she is feeling in the story as a narrator would, as this transfers these feelings to her in reality. Feelings of strong desire can be repeated so that a touch can become electric.
6. The story ends as the physical dimension takes over from the verbalising of the story and the two characters make love.

I suggested this idea to a couple that I was counselling. They complained of a predictable, unexciting love life and desperately wanted a change. The man found it difficult to communicate his feelings and found it hard to increase passion in the relationship. They tried my idea but the husband found he was not creative enough to just make up a story as he went along. In their case I suggested two alternatives. Firstly, I suggested that the wife tell the story to the man the first couple of times, so he could enjoy it and catch on to both how it was done and the themes she wanted. Secondly, I suggested that he make up a sketch of a story and jot down the main points so that he could remember it later on, when he would tell it to his wife.

The idea worked for them in a fascinating way. She dreamed up this incredibly sexy story of her and her (in reality non-existent) twin sister where they were both rich and beautiful, and how they both craved her man and his body. She however, won her man's affections over her sister through her deep, instant connection with her man. The boundaries can be determined by the couple but in this case the man really enjoyed the story and got the idea. What was interesting was that she really enjoyed telling the stories and so they started sharing the story telling. She found she liked being in control of the story plot and the pace of the development of the foreplay. She became turned on as she verbalised the intensity of the feelings of her character in the story.

Over a short period of time they learned to build desire outside of their bedroom as one partner promised the other, "Have I got a story for you tonight! You are just going to love it." Furthermore, it made their love life more exciting even when they did not tell stories and it also increased the foreplay in other times as well.

This idea may not be for everyone but the concept illustrates how important it is for one to make love to the person's mind and not just the body. It seems to work best with people who are naturally imaginative and creative. Both partners can enjoy the physical dimension so much more when the man understands how to make love to a woman's mind first. So next time your man wants to make love, tell him to put on a blindfold while you tell him an adult bedtime story!

The physical dimension can be enjoyed by both partners so much more when the man understands how to make love to a woman's mind first.

8. There Used To Be More Sexual Play Outside The Bedroom

There is a common tendency in relationships that the longer the couple are together the less touching occurs between the two, especially outside of lovemaking. This is a tragedy because as soon as the man starts to touch, it cannot be appreciated because the woman thinks, "I know what he wants". Lovemaking and even touching itself can degenerate into a chore for women that can act as a barrier blocking a woman's need for intimacy. At the same time a man's fantasy of his lady desiring him is also stifled and sex can lose the power, enchantment and closeness that it has the potential to give.

Think back to when you were first in love with your lover. The physical display of that love would have been clearly evident to all. Both of you would have that primary focus on the other, as you gazed into each other's eyes. Both of you would touch each other freely both privately and in public. Watch some young lovers sometime to see how they are uninhibited. Maybe you will say, "I couldn't act like that with my partner". But why not? Perhaps you used to but what has changed? Possibly only time and marriage. The point is that your relationship will most likely be better and more romantic if you touched a lot more. By touching each other outside of lovemaking you are bringing romance back into your relationship and teaching your partner to fulfil your need for intimacy. You also remove the element of lovemaking being a chore because now that your needs are met you are now in a good position to fulfil your partner's needs. Not only that, but all of this touching over the past couple of days has made you crazy with desire now that you know he is touching you for the very sake of wanting to touch you and connect with you and not because he is trying to give you the hint that he wants something from you. Try all sorts of touching such as stroking his head, rubbing his back, pinching his bottom or caressing his crutch. Any sort of sexual play that both of you know will not necessarily always be a preamble to making love falls into this category of touch. In the last chapter we will talk about the science of touch and how important it is in establishing romantic connection.

By touching each other outside of lovemaking you are bringing romance back into your relationship and teaching your partner to fulfil your need for intimacy.

Talk to your partner about it but also lead by example. If you wish to be touched more, then start touching **him** more. As your touching becomes more spontaneous, natural and expected, your romance, both outside and under the sheets will begin to explode.

9. There Used To Be An Emphasis On Passion

Another tendency in long-term relationships is that passion gives way to routine. Another reason romance dies in a relationship is because passion dies. When a couple are first in love they wish they could kiss all night, and sometimes do. When romance is at its peak, passion is at its peak. Every area of the relationship becomes filled with passion. There are passionate embraces when greeting or parting, passionate kissing and cuddling whenever, and passionate lovemaking rather than mechanical sex in bed. Another part of this passion is seen in the length of foreplay, which is usually, on average, longer and more intense in the earlier, more romantic stages of the relationship.

When romance is at its peak, passion is at its peak.

How your relationship scores on the passionate scale may well parallel how it scores on the romantic scale provided the passion is two-way. Some couples fall into the habit of very rarely kissing passionately under the sheets or kissing at all for that matter. It can be easy for a man to fall into the habit of short foreplay and little passion, but once reminded a man can learn to enjoy both the journey and the destination. Try reintroducing the emphasis of passion back into your lives and see how it can rekindle the flame of romance. Teach your man the art and importance of foreplay and how to make the whole experience more passionate. Let your hearts return to when you first fell in love and see how much you enjoy it.

10. There Used To Be More Fun

Back then it was seen as fun, but now it is probably looked upon as childishness. Well, if there is one thing about children it is they have a lot of fun. Why? Because they are children and are not afraid of being embarrassed at having fun, or playing around. They don't have any images to maintain or expectations to live up to. Their occupation is having fun. If you were young when you fell in love you probably still carry with you an element of fun loving playfulness, possibly even childishness at times, in your relationship. It is not uncommon for even old people who fall in love to catch this fun element again. The whole point is to analyse your own relationship and see whether it fits into the category of "fun loving" or "stiff and starchy".

It may be that both you and your partner need to rediscover fun and childishness by becoming a child again, especially in your bedroom. Give yourself a licence some times to leave the adult at the door to your bedroom and only allow the child in, that you have recaptured. There need be no embarrassments or images to maintain here except an insatiable one. Learn to enjoy the fun of romp and frolic, play and wrestle, not just as a child but as an adult child.

> *Give yourself a licence some times to leave the adult at the door to your bedroom and only allow the child in, that you have recaptured.*

Remember that romance is fun and playing with your spouse introduces a relaxed, happy and exciting dimension into your relationship.

11. Variety

Variety is the spice of our sex lives as well as life in general. Another part of new romantic relationships is the eagerness of partners to explore different positions, and different aspects of their sexuality and lovemaking. Ask yourself the question of how many different positions you have made love in, in the past twelve months? Have you got to the place where you respond that you forgot there was more than one? The number of positions will not of itself make your love life fulfilling but it is often true that long term relationships that degenerate into ruts often seem to be in a set routine when it comes to sex.

By adding variety to your sex life you add that little bit of surprise, mystery, newness, change in aggressiveness or passiveness, change in visual and touch stimuli and something that is not easily predictable; most of which can also be seen as elements of romance.

It is the predictability of making love that women often complain about, if not to their partners, to themselves deep down. It is as if you think, "Oh no, it's going to be as exciting as the last time". The predictable element engenders a negative attitude towards sex in general. If this attitude is cultivated over many years one could imagine how strongly entrenched it could become and how hard it would be to escape from. But by adding variety and having a more positive attitude you can break the cycle. Earlier we talked about filling one's mind with positive, romantic thoughts at bedtime to crowd out the negative ones. But in order to wind down a little more before bedtime you may need to work on your attitude before you hop into bed. Sometimes a little, relaxing luxury before bedtime is just what's needed.

It is the predictability of making love that women often complain about, if not to their partners, to themselves deep down.

Either sipping a hot drink or soaking in a hot bath might just be the key to changing your attitudes and filling bedtime with more desire and positives. Certainly a greater preparation time before sex can extend foreplay and give you time to get more in the mood, so that you can gain more enjoyment out of the most intimate time of the day.

It is because men can be ready for sexual intercourse instantaneously that many of them think that a woman can be too. Many men can become frustrated when a woman doesn't show the same level of immediate readiness. Such a man needs to be educated that a woman needs to be prepared more for making love. Indeed, the man that understands this secret, causes lovemaking for his lady to be far more pleasurable and desirable, which consequently makes it more pleasurable for him. By preparing his spouse throughout the day and hours beforehand a man can inject a large dose of romance into his love life. So try not only adding variety to your sex life and preparing yourself positively for romance in bed. Try educating him about the importance of preparation. Continuing the theme of preparation, this leads us to the next comparison of why romance initially used to be so good under the sheets.

12. There Used To Be The Right Time And Conditions For The Female Erection To Take Place.

Are males the only ones that have erections? Certainly not! It's just the size that's different! You see, men's genitalia are just so visible and the changes under men's erection are so dramatic, that they are the ones that get all the attention when it comes to erections. It's just that women's erections are more subtle in contrast to men's. But this doesn't make them any less important than men's.

A woman's erection occurs on two levels, both physiologically and psychologically, yet the two are so intertwined and inseparable. The male erection is the name given to the changes that take place in the male body to allow him to penetrate the woman. Similarly, the female erection is the name given to the changes that take place in a woman's body to not only be ready and accepting but also desirous of penetration. Physiologically, the female erection consists of a change in blood flow and blood rush to the genitalia, the clitoris especially. It also consists of an erection of the nipples at times, and a firming up of the clitoris. Furthermore, it is the vagina preparing itself with lubrication to enable reception of the penis. It is also the increase in sensitivity of the woman's total sexuality. But it is more than that. Psychologically, it is a setting one's self on the path of arousal, it is giving license to enjoy one's self and one's body, and giving permission to be aroused. A good erection for a woman has both these qualities, physical readiness and an appetite for mind sex.

The important difference in erections between men and women is the fact that a man's erection normally can be immediate, whereas a woman's erection is usually nowhere near as quick. The process just takes a little longer for a woman, so that she can get more out of lovemaking, which allows her to enjoy the whole journey of lovemaking and not just the destination.

A couple came to me one time with the problem that the wife was just not enjoying sex as she previously did. She wanted to, and she found her partner attractive but the physical responses were just not strong enough for her. This was in stark contrast to their early love life when her responses were overwhelmingly fulfilling. The couple's problem was that they didn't understand the female erection. Over the years, the length of time they spent in each sexual act had diminished greatly and this short cut and effortless lifestyle was meeting her man's needs but had killed his wife's enjoyment.

By explaining to the couple about the female erection, both learned the importance of committing greater time, planning variety, building the excitement and the raising of the priority of their love life. It is true that sometimes when a woman complains of the lack of her physical sensitivity in her love life, it can be traced to the lack of awareness of the female erection. In the age of fast food, fast lifestyle and fast everything, fast sex is just not as compatible with a woman's satisfaction as some may wish. But if sex could be reduced to such a level, would it not reduce sex to that of a chore, something to get over and done with as quickly as possible? Indeed for too many women in long term relationships this can be how they are forced to view it.

> *Sometimes when a woman complains of the lack of her physical sensitivity in her love life, it can be traced to the lack of awareness of the female erection.*

Male impotence and male erection problems in general receive a great deal of attention. It consumes a vast amount of resources and receives much publicity and yet it is arguable that a greater number of women suffer from female impotence, or lack of erection and yet what resources are involved in assisting in this area? Fortunately, the solution may be as simple as a commitment to lengthen the time of foreplay and to educate men of the importance of preparing a woman for lovemaking, extending foreplay and tease before the couple even reach the bedroom. It is like sprinkling the whole relationship with the rain of foreplay, damming up the sensations to be released in flood like proportions at the time of lovemaking. Now that is romance!

When telling a man that a woman needs more time before penetration and more foreplay, a man may find it hard to understand and consider it very nebulous and unessential. But when a man understands it in terms of necessity by comparing it with his own erection, he can understand **why** it is so important. He can visualise it and comprehend it more in a sequential cause and effect basis, the way a man's mind is used to working with information. A man has to understand that sex without foreplay for a woman is like intercourse without an erection for a man. When a man appreciates this analogy he begins to understand the importance of making sure he has given her time so she is aroused and desires to receive him. In turn the man enjoys giving his partner more enjoyment, this turns him on more and he finds his effort has increased his enjoyment. Intimate long-term relationships are like that. The more **both partners** give, the more satisfying it is for both. Such an understanding can take extra effort, but it has the effect of aligning the couple's sexual compatibility and satisfaction.

> *A man has to understand that sex without foreplay for a woman is like intercourse without an erection for a man.*

In summary, as far as romance in relation to sex goes, it seems the single biggest factor that kills romance is that foreplay always seems to decrease in long term relationships. By putting the formula in reverse one can say that to revive romance in long term relationships in regard to the sexual relationship of the couple, time and effort should be paid to increasing foreplay (which creates the conditions for the female erection to take place).

That concludes our first section on comparison to the early, romantic aspects of intimate relationships. Let's turn now to some other vital areas that can dramatically inject romance into the bedroom.

B. THE PRIMARY MALE FANTASY

Back in chapter four I referred to Warren Farrell's statement of men's primary fantasy - "access to as many beautiful women without the risk of rejection." To state it more in the positive, instead of "without the risk of rejection", we could say "with the women going crazy with desire for him". If a woman, whom a man is extremely attracted to, is desirous of that man, **and shows it**, the risk of the man being rejected is removed. So an extension of a man's primary fantasy is the woman wanting him and showing him aggressively that she wants him. A man can feel in control of the situation if the woman is chasing him. Naturally the effect is heightened when the woman has a strong desire for him exclusively and no one else. Every man wishes and fantasises he had more sex appeal than any other man, so that women would just swoon wherever he walked.

So what do men's fantasies have to do with you and romance? Well first of all, if you can meet your man's fantasy then he will be in a better position to meet your needs and fantasies. If your love life becomes one of fantasy fulfilment you are going to have great romance under the sheets. The logical conclusion is that generally, men want women to be more aggressive, more desirous of them under the sheets. This means men want women to sometimes initiate, lead and take control in making love.

> *The logical conclusion is that generally, men want women to be more aggressive, more desirous of them under the sheets.*

This is why it is so important for you both to have the right attitude when you begin to make love. I believe the author of *A Skilled Lover Reveals All* in Cleo Magazine June 1990 got it right when he said, "It's desire that turns you on... If a woman does have a perfect body but lies there like a log, it takes four seconds to forget about that body." On the other hand when a woman shows desire, and actively participates in making love, the whole experience is intensified for both partners.

Try being more aggressive and ask your man how he enjoys it. You just may begin to fulfil his fantasies and connect him to you like nothing else. How long has it been since you did a strip tease for your man? What about the last time you seduced him when making love was the furthermost thing on his mind? (Is that possible?) Try adding more seduction to your relationship outside the bedroom and watch the romantic response from your partner. Look for the effects on your love life as well. Be bold and aggressive so that when your man watches television, practise running your hand up the inside of his thigh slowly, just to remind him you are there. Try it for a couple of weeks and notice how your partner will often copy it by caressing you in a similar way.

One aspect about prostitution is that a woman becomes sexually aggressive for a man. That is the service the customer pays for. A prostitute who lies there, does nothing and acts as though she were uninterested, soon runs out of customers. It might be that your man would appreciate you being aggressive now and again in the bedroom, but you might never know if you never ask and he is comfortable in telling you.

C. WHAT TURNS MEN AND WOMEN ON?

The most important answer to this question is simply, "totally different things." When people don't understand this most basic concept, frustration occurs because both try to turn the other on, ***the way they want themselves to be turned on.*** By both partners being educated on what their partners enjoy, frustration can be removed as both become fulfilled by different actions. It's like looking for buried treasure. You can look in all the wrong places all your life. But once you have the treasure map, it's easy, just as long as you understand it and follow the instructions. It's always easy when you know how.

Remember the caveman's primary sense was sight. The window to his arousal is through his eyes. Consider the primary male fantasy of a woman having desire for her man. It is when he sees that desire in her eyes, and in her body that a man cannot help but get aroused. So when a man says, "I want you," or "I want to make love to you," he is in fact mirroring his own desires in how he is turned on. He often takes the initiative just as he wishes his partner would. He finds it easy to take off his clothes, just as he wishes she would be aggressive and be filled with desire to take off her clothes. It is a mirroring of this all important visual arousal that shows how many a man tries to duplicate seduction when it comes to arousing his spouse. All he knows is how it works for ***him***.

> *When a man says, "I want you," or "I want to make love to you," he is in fact mirroring his own desires in how he is turned on.*

It is this physical, visual window to his own arousal that a man often arms himself with when he searches out intimacy in new relationships, in spite of the fact that he may have been unsuccessful with this approach in the past. He becomes so hungry for his own needs to be fulfilled, so overwhelmed with the possibility of physical satisfaction in any potential relationship that friction occurs when a potential partner's needs conflict with his own. His advances often become a mirror that express his own desires, even though he may expend a great deal of time, effort and money on those advances. This can be seen in some men who become obsessed with building a perfect, physical body and dream that this is all it will take to attract women. I am not discrediting the benefits for anyone going to the gym and working out. What I am saying is that when it becomes a man's *sole* attempt at attracting women it merely mirrors a man's orientation to the physical and visual. This explains why a man would rather spend a year body building than attending a course on communication, relationship enrichment, romance and understanding women's needs. Yet the later would probably be far more successful for a long-term relationship.

Take for instance John, who hasn't been educated about the differences in men and women. He wants to turn his partner on. So what does he do? After Mary has got into bed, like a true caveman he rips off his clothes and stands at the foot of the bed waiting for her to notice him. Because he is turned on by the visual, he logically expects that she is turned on the same way. Eventually he gets her attention but her response is not as he expected. Whereas he would be instantly aroused by the sheer sight of her naked form, she merely glances at him, hardly even noticing his state of undress and isn't aroused at all by what she sees. Thinking his uncovered manhood should be enough he now feels belittled by his partner's apparent rejection of his masculinity.

The next night Mary wants to be intimate with John. But she reaches for him verbally, the way she wishes John would connect with her. John is occupied with his own interests he has withdrawn into. He now feels smothered with Mary's constant questions, which are meaningless to him and just a bother. He doesn't realise it is an attempt for Mary to connect with him which is the window to her arousal. She is attempting to get him to express his undying love for her, to show her how devoted he is to her and how nothing else is as important to him as her. But it doesn't work. Her prodding is misunderstood. He is already hurt because of the rejection he felt from the night before. So the misunderstanding and frustration continue, even though John and Mary love each other and both have tried to initiate intimacy. Does it sound familiar at all?

The solution is that the vicious cycle has to be broken by at least one partner. Both partners need to be educated about what their mate's specific needs are and how they can fulfil them. Both need to appreciate how the other wants to be turned on, and how this varies from their own desires. This can be a key to bringing passion back into the bedroom. The most difficult step is for each to give up the priority of their own needs being met in the way they desire. But once that step is taken, each experiences a new satisfaction as they become involved with the other person's excitement. This in turn is fuelled with reciprocal behaviour as each finds new enjoyment in not only having their own needs met but meeting their partner's needs.

But our partners will not know unless they have it explained to them. This is why writing down our needs, our desires and sharing the list with our spouse is so important. It is connecting the effort with desire, so that there is no wasted effort and no desire that is not met. A man that understands your desires, connects with you totally and turns you on the way you want to be turned on. What could be more romantic?

It is connecting the effort with desire, so that there is no wasted effort and no desire that is not met.

D. ROMANTIC TIMING

One of the pitfalls for the modern, sexual couple can be an expectation of wanting achievement just as the sex manual records it. With such a written plethora on sexuality, and a strong emphasis on a performance mentality, it is possible for a couple's sexual compatibility to actually be inhibited, unless it is specifically geared towards the individuals concerned. With an emphasis on certain types of orgasms, encouragement for certain gymnastic positions and an education that makes a person think they are missing out on everything unless they follow the manual to the letter, couples can be excused for being left sexually bewildered.

Although the general pathways to climaxes are physically and biologically set, there has been a trend to emphasise the physical dos and don'ts to the exclusion of mood. By limiting a couple's sex education totally to the sex manuals that stress the physical ins and outs of the act itself, a couple can miss the importance of romance, mind sex, creating desire, and how these can also colour the climactic process.

Simultaneous Orgasms

Sometimes the pressure of attempting to follow the instructions can override the pleasure of the process itself and obstruct the beauty of natural discovery. For example, there is sometimes too great an emphasis on simultaneous orgasms. Simultaneous orgasms can be a binding expression of love, but some couples structure their love life as if this was the only form of sex. What I have found when a couple rigidly organise their sex life so that every time it happens, it happens simultaneously, is that it places pressure in all the wrong areas. One couple I knew just did not consider any other possibility - they just assumed that *every* time they made love they both would climax at the same time. This mind set can lead to three problem areas as follows.

1. It does not allow for differences in sex drives.

As soon as there is a difference in the frequency of need, either one person is coerced into having an orgasm when they do not really want one, or the other is frustrated by having to put their need on hold. The solution of course is to have a more flexible arrangement where simultaneous orgasms are welcome when both prefer them, but to also have times when only one partner is indulged to climax. Romantic couples are understanding of their partner's sexual appetite, even when the other partner may not be hungry for it.

Some people run their relationship not romantically but on the basis of sexual manipulation. They will only give into sexual favours if they can bargain a deal for their own ends. For one partner to expect that they should make love only when they alone want it can be seen as selfish, but also denies the fact that two entirely unique people form the relationship. Because of the differences in sex drives many make themselves available but only grudgingly. In other words, we say yes but we take away all emotion, desire, feeling and dual stimulation and then expect our partner to "go ahead and enjoy" themselves. It becomes only one step up from masturbation where we say our body will be present but it "will depend upon your ability to stimulate yourself". It's our non-verbal communication, which screams out, "Go ahead, but you won't have my mind, my desire, my all".

> *For one partner to expect that they should make love only when they alone want it can be seen as selfish, but also denies the fact that two entirely unique people form the relationship.*

Remember back a few pages under the section entitled the primary male fantasy where we talked about the importance of responsiveness, and how unresponsiveness was a complete turn off for men. This withholding of ourselves can be a killer when it comes to intimacy, bonding, satisfaction and keeping interest. To correct the problem of the woman who complains her man is bored with her, the woman can often arouse his interest in her again by beginning to respond again and thereby recreate that primary male fantasy.

This point is demonstrated to the extreme both by prostitution but also by pornographic films. A prostitute to keep customers coming back must respond to them and at least pretend to be enjoying herself. So too, the actors in pornographic films must pretend they are constantly on the virtual verge of climax in an attempt to create the primary male fantasy. You do not have to scream every time your partner touches you as there are many varied ways you can show response. The important thing is that you are aware of the importance of responding and committing your mind and body to your partner. There is something deep down inside a man's ego that sends him wild when he is given clear signs that his lady is receiving sexual pleasure from him. Could it be possible that some men subconsciously seek out an affair to convince themselves that they are still capable of inciting a strong response from a woman? I believe it is worth thinking about carefully.

2. Rigidly making every sexual encounter simultaneous can put pressure on one party at one time or another to fake an orgasm.

If simultaneous orgasms are expected and yet the desire is not there, rather than denying one's spouse, one can always be faced with the pressure of attempting to manufacture something, which may just simply not be there. The intention to fake may arise out of the best of motives such as not wanting to hurt the other party, yet an introduction to faking can lead to destructive forces being released into the relationship. Pretending an orgasm is not only deceptive but also cheating oneself, not to mention the accumulative, compounded problem of stopping the faking after repetitive episodes. Some may prefer to fake it than to say no but the long term effect can result in boredom with, or even resentful of, sex or to become estranged emotionally as well as sexually from one's partner. All this happens at the same time that one's partner thinks everything is fine. The best solution is not to be tied to simultaneous orgasms every time but still to enjoy the loving of the moment regardless of the climactic outcome.

> *The best solution is not to be tied to simultaneous orgasms every time but still to enjoy the loving of the moment regardless of the climactic outcome*

Sexual inflexibility in many forms can act as an insurmountable block to romance. In contrast sexual flexibility can smooth over a couple's sexual hiccups before they can become disasters. Some people become so restricted that they can only climax under a special set of prerequisites. They have to have either a certain position or be stimulated in a certain way in order to reach orgasm. Sometimes a person's inflexible temperament can be reflected in their inflexible sexual routines, so much so that they can only live under a completely ordered and charted sexual plan. In such an environment, spontaneity may be seen as a threat or intolerable rather than a refreshing change.

It is possible for any of us to be slaves to such an inflexible routine without us even being aware of it. For instance, over the years many couples in long term relationships with the same partner build up comfortable, safe, "flawless" ways of having sex. This is an **emotionally** "safe sex" approach. It is safe to the individual because it has worked hundreds of times before and so they stay with it because they know it will work again for them. This "safe sex" security blanket may be protecting and comfortable, but it can also be very unexciting, very drab and very boring. Liberating one's self to trying new techniques, new positions, new experiences once in a while may mean that they will not be successful every time, but they will inject a rejuvenation, a vigour and even an adolescent, risk taking attitude that may result in a freshness in one's sex life.

If you have found you have preferred the same routines of sex for years, and perhaps are even feeling a little stale, then maybe it is time to take a chance and try something new once in a while. You may find it liberating, romantic, refreshing and opening up a totally new smorgasbord of options that become available for you to choose from. Do not stop the old ways and replace them with something new. Just simply add some new ways to the old every so often so you can have the best of both worlds. Remember that it may be that the old boring ways best suit your lifestyle, your personalities, your sexual needs and desires.

3. Simultaneous orgasms every time can diminish the effect of the orgasm by removing the focus of pleasure to concentrating on stimulating one's partner.

Some people find it hard to concentrate on anything for very long. Men often complain that they have a battle to win over their partner's mind because during lovemaking women come up with such statements as, "Did you put the rubbish out tonight?", "What was that noise?", or "When is the electricity bill due?" Other people find that it requires the power of strong concentration in order to reach a climax. This not only illustrates the importance for a man to understand how to be skilled at mind sex (preparing a woman's mind for sex) but also underlines the fact that sometimes a partner's rise to orgasm (or lack of it) can be a distraction in itself to one's concentration. There are of course variables from person to person as what one person finds distracting another may find arousing. Some people get very turned on when they hear their partner's moans of delight, which in turn can catapult them over the rise of ecstasy. The key is to think and talk about what distracts you and your partner and remove them, and add what turns you both on.

When the male orgasm takes place after the female, it has the benefit of sometimes ensuring a better afterglow experience for the woman. Because the pleasure of the male orgasm is terminated abruptly in contrast to the female pleasure, which falls away more gently, a delayed male orgasm can mean a better matching of the afterglow time.

Contrast the graphs below and notice the **shared** heightened pleasure after the female climax.

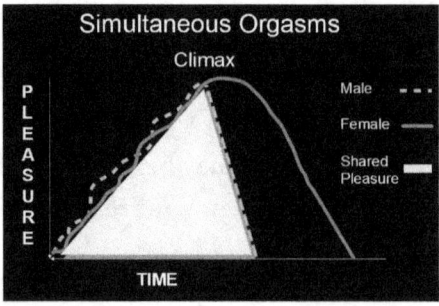

The total **shared** pleasure is short lived.

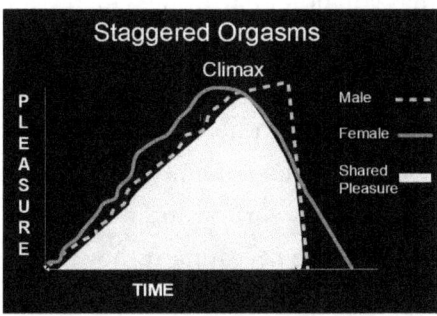

The total *shared* pleasure is extended.

A further benefit of the female orgasm taking place before the male is the opportunity it presents for multiple female orgasms. It is because of the sudden termination of the erection for the male, once his orgasm has taken place that makes simultaneous orgasms difficult for multiple female orgasms. On the other hand, in a staggered approach, a man can still stimulate his partner after she has climaxed if she wishes to continue her pleasure.

E. HOW TO COMMUNICATE YOUR LIKES AND DISLIKES

It is true that most women wished their men knew intuitively what their needs were and how they would like them fulfilled. It is unfortunate though, that most men don't know intuitively what their wives wished they did, or that so many women don't take any positive steps to communicate their sexual likes and dislikes. It is far easier and practical for women to learn to communicate their needs rather than to teach men to be mind readers.

It is far easier and practical for women to learn to communicate their needs rather than to teach men to be mind readers.

One way is to discuss together frankly and openly what you like done to you and what you don't like done. Open your man up by asking what his likes and dislikes are, what he wants more of, what he wants less of, in your sex life. Talk about and accept each other's fantasies so you can both learn where the other's desires lie. Target areas such as initiating foreplay, what builds your desire and turns you on, talking during lovemaking, romance, variety and needs after climax.

Some couples find it more revealing if they both write a list of what they like and want more of in their bedroom, and then swap the list with their partner. Then they can discuss together the ideas, taking turns from each list. However you do it is not the issue, the point is that some way or another you have to discuss your sexual desires and needs with your partner so that both partners are clear. Sometimes the only thing that can be stopping sexual oneness is the fact that your man doesn't know your actual needs. He may **think** he knows, he can spend much time and effort trying his best to fulfil what he ***thinks*** is right, when in reality he is a long way from the mark. Make sure your man is channelling his efforts into the bull's eye, anything else is not fair to you or him.

> *Make sure your man is channelling his efforts into the bull's eye, anything else is not fair to you or him.*

Desires and wants can change from time to time and it is not always possible for you to discuss these issues every time before you make love. So how do you convey to your man each time whether he is hitting the bull's eye or not? What I suggest is that you and your man get used to what I call the "indicator and accelerator". This provides a non-verbal indicator to a man of whether he is getting it right or not in a very non-threatening way and is ideal for women who find it hard to convey verbally their sexual likes in detail.

Often men are left in the dark, hunting for signs of response from their lovers. They don't know whether this time they are doing it right or not. A simple indicator can be for you to squeeze your partner's little finger when he gets it right and when you want him to continue what he is doing. You may like to substitute an ear or some other part of his body within reach that you won't hurt by squeezing. By letting go when he displeases you or doesn't do very much for you, your partner gets the idea immediately to try something different. By continuing what he is doing when he feels the squeeze, he can intensify the pleasure. In this way the indicator becomes an accelerator because the harder you squeeze the more he intensifies what you desire. Men also desire the challenge of getting you to squeeze in response to their efforts because they don't have to guess, they know for sure that you are turned on when you squeeze, and that also turns them on more than anything else.

Once you and your man have caught on to the "indicator and accelerator" you will find it an invaluable aid in lovemaking. There is no lost time and energy but it is all spent directly on what you want. It also affirms your lover when he does it right which is also important.

> *Once you and your man have caught on to the "indicator and accelerator" you will find it an invaluable aid in lovemaking.*

F. THE LITTLE THINGS COUNT

It's good to remember that it's the little things that often bring big results. Every now and again it's worth setting the best scene possible for an intimate encounter in your bedroom with your partner. We have looked at issues such as communication, and getting your man to prepare you for bedtime, preparing yourself, the importance of keeping a positive attitude and a whole range of other points. But there are small physical things you can do to inject romance into lovemaking. Candles or soft lighting, incense or perfume, and soft music can set the scene so well. It takes very little effort but can make so much difference. You may find a simple thing like introducing more lace or lingerie, and wearing it for an hour or two before you go to bed, not only sets the mood for you, but also wets your partner's appetite.

Vouchers these days are commonplace for all sorts of things. Vouchers can give you a credit to spend at the time you want to. Some couples also find giving one another vouchers for special activities also very romantic and exciting. You can write out your own vouchers as you would an IOU. Or you can draw up professional looking ones on a personal computer. You can make a standard one and then fill in the individual details to suit what you want. You can date it or leave it open. Here are a few examples.

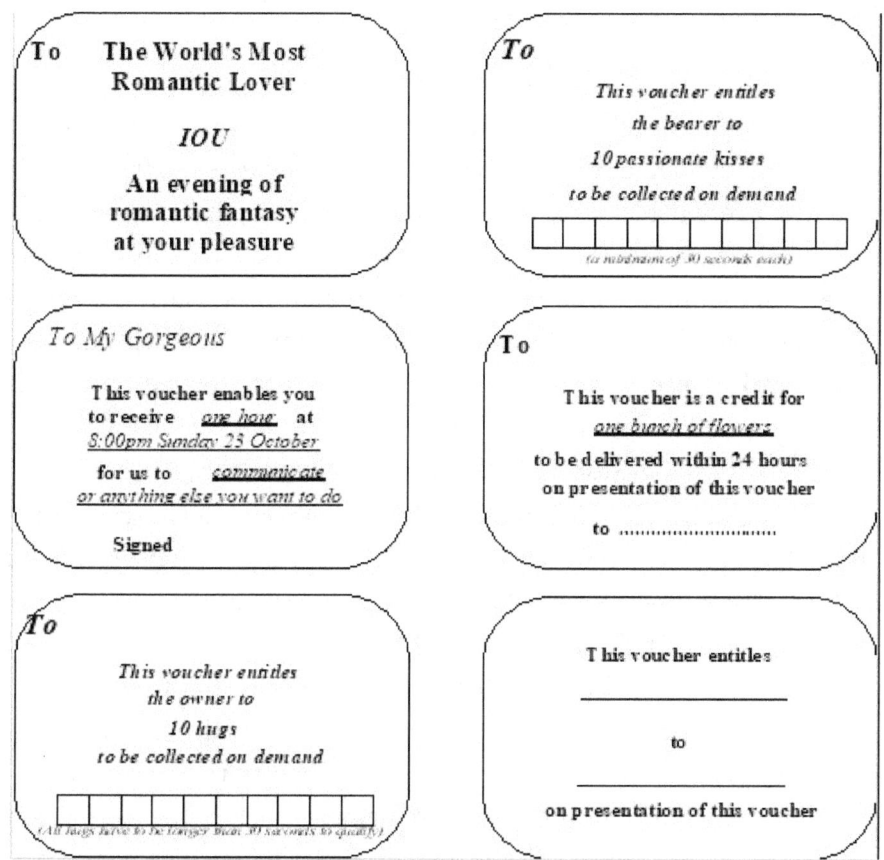

These vouchers are designed to be structured to the couple's individual needs. The scope is virtually endless, being only limited by your desires and imagination. Vouchers aren't meant to take the place of every need being fulfilled, but they can be used for those special times to add romance and charm. They can also be used when the receiver wants them or needs them most. The whole idea, in keeping with the ideals of fairness, is that the couple swap an equal amount of vouchers, so that both give and both receive. Vouchers can also act as a reminder to your man as to what are your romantic needs. A couple can have a lot of fun and satisfaction if they are allowed to fill in their own vouchers and then give them back to their partners to date, think about and plan for. It's also another avenue in which a couple can communicate their needs, desires and romantic fantasies to each other.

G. What Do You *Think* About Romance?

So far we have talked a lot about the mind. We have talked about the internal switch in the mind that needs to be switched to the on position to appreciate pleasure. We have talked about the mind as being the greatest sex organ in a woman's body. We have looked at how guilt for instance can blunt the mind to sexual and romantic pleasure and desire. We have seen the importance of focusing the mind on accepting pleasure in order to receive the potential pleasure. But one question needs to be answered clearly in order for a woman to enjoy romance under the sheets. That question is, "What do you really **believe** about sex?"

All of us build up beliefs about a whole range of topics as we journey through our lives. In a great number of cases our beliefs are forged through negative experiences which can often result in negative, irrational beliefs about all sorts of areas. A kid gets beaten up at school only once and then he suffers from anxiety whenever he has to go back to school. But that anxiety comes from a belief forged through personal experience that school is not safe. The original kid who beat him up has long left the school but the anxiety remains whenever the association cuts in. It happens automatically. Sometimes it happens in a situation where his conscious mind doesn't even make the connection between feeling unsafe now and 30 years ago when he was beat up at school. The feelings of anxiety just flood in as if all by themselves and he feels terribly anxious, paralysingly so.

This is why sexual therapists take a sexual history of their clients. Negative sexual experiences linger. They may not always linger in the conscious mind but they linger just the same. The negative experience itself might have even been forgotten, but the feelings attached to it jump out at the most irritating times. But also in the mind, the brain has formulated certain beliefs about those negative sexual experiences in an attempt to safeguard the person in the future. Sometimes it minimises harm to the person for a while but often it holds them back at a later date. For example, a negative sexual experience might stop a young woman from having another intimate relationship ever again.

She might form a belief that "you can't trust men" or something similar. Every time a man gets close to her she might end up sabotaging the relationship or starting a fight with him. It's simply a defence mechanism which can operate below the level of conscious understanding. But while the belief might act to protect a woman from being hurt by another man ever again, it might also rob her of her potential future pleasure and happiness. You see, defence mechanisms not only serve to keep the bad out, they also keep the good out.

Even if a woman has never had a negative sexual experience, she could still have received negative sexual education. It could have been overt negative education from one of her own parents or some other authority figure when she was young. Or it could have been a more subtle, non-verbal education such as looks of horror when speaking about a woman who was known to be overtly sexually active. If you grew up in a sexually conservative, rigid household you may hold negative beliefs about your own sexuality you are not even aware you hold. Especially, if you grew up in a ***religiously*** conservative, rigid home, you will probably have unhealthy beliefs in regards to romance, sex and pleasure. Guilt in particular, will most likely be a huge issue which will work to minimise sexual pleasure in your life.

So how do you find out if you have these irrational beliefs in your own life working against your pleasure and happiness? You could see a sex therapist who might be able to discover what some of these irrational beliefs are that are operating in your life. Usually, wherever there is a fear, an anxiety or you are getting negative outcomes in your sexual experiences, there is a good chance you have an irrational belief driving these negative outcomes. Below I have included a sexual beliefs inventory for you to use as a starting point which is designed to reveal the severity to which you might believe of the ten most common irrational sexual beliefs. This is a good questionnaire to take to start exploring what you really think about romance under the sheets. Before you start, you might want to take a copy of the answer sheet and have your partner fill in the inventory as well. Then if you are game you can show each other your results and discuss what this means and how it affects your sex life.

SEXUAL BELIEFS INVENTORY (QUESTIONS)

1. I don't think I should have to communicate my sexual needs to my partner - he or she should be sensitive or intelligent enough to know them

2. The primary focus of sex for me is the tension release

3. It can be embarrassing if my spouse watches me get undressed

4. It is OK to experiment with sex with your partner as long as both are comfortable with it and it is controlled by love

5. It's a terrible thing to go for long periods without sex

6. If my partner rejects me I don't feel loved

7. Gasping noises, heavy breathing and facial grimaces associated with climax are embarrassing or should be minimised

8. Too much sex education can spoil it

9. It is naïve to think that women can enjoy sex as much as men

10. Couples in de facto relationships always seem to have better sex than those who have been married a long time

11. I like to tell my partner exactly what I prefer almost every time

12. I virtually never forget about or ignore my partner's sexual needs or pleasure

13. I sometimes feel guilty after having had mutually enjoyable sex with my partner

14. I catch myself responding sexually at times before I realise it

15. If a couple are having problems with their sex life it is important to resolve it as soon as possible even if they are both getting on anyway

16. I never feel angry when my partner rejects my sexual advances

17. The more active I am the better the climax

18. All that one needs to have a good sex life is to do what comes naturally

19. A man's sex drive will always be stronger than any woman's

20. Sex certainly does get better the longer you are in a relationship

21. I wish my partner would do different things to what he or she normally does but I don't want to tell him or her in case his or her feelings are hurt

22. I never find myself preoccupied and obsessed with sex a lot of the time

23. I don't get pleasure out of sex even when I climax

24. I sometimes find myself unable to enjoy very much the buildup before climax

25. Sex never gets forgotten about by me in my relationship

26. I don't feel loved unless my sexual life is going well

27. I enjoy or am comfortable with only one or two positions

28. Problems shouldn't occur in sex if you just relax and get it right anatomically

29. Women can get just as much out of sex as men

30. Sex doesn't have to get in a rut after years of being in a relationship

31. I would always communicate immediately when my partner does something sexually that I don't like

32. I don't expect my partner should always be there for me sexually if they don't feel like it themselves

33. The main purpose of sex is procreation

34. I think people are naturally inhibited about sex until they are taught otherwise

35. I never seem to be far too busy to have a great sex life

36. Sex has never been the most important thing to me in my relationship

37. I am hardly ever the passive partner in sex

38. You don't have to learn anything about sex; you should just let nature take its course

39. Women have just as good an orgasm as men

40. I never fear that my sex life will worsen over time

41. If my partner doesn't please me sexually I make sure I let them know

42. I find I have an overwhelming urge to have sex every day

43. I never feel embarrassed if my partner stares at me when I am naked

44. I am a naturally curious person sexually

45. I always get frustrated if I go for weeks or longer without sex

46. I can be perfectly satisfied at times if cuddling doesn't lead to sex

47. I find it difficult to respond straight away to sexual stimulation

48. You need to know all the ins and outs about sex to have a good sex life

49. Sex is really only for men

50. One's sex life naturally deteriorates the longer one is in a long term relationship

51. It's not romantic or practical if I have to tell my partner exactly what I want during sex

52. I have never found myself getting agitated if I think I am going to miss out on sex

53. I don't have a problem with examining my genitals with a mirror

54. When I am having sex I am comfortable with just letting go and enjoying the experience

55. Sex doesn't figure in my top ten things to do

56. I never fight with my partner over me not having enough sex or a particular type of sex

57. I am comfortable with enticing or seducing my partner

58. I needed lots of sex education; I never innately possessed the skills of a good lover

59. It would be very difficult for a woman to go for years without having sex

60. Sex definitely doesn't improve with age

61. I am not afraid to redirect my partner if it is not having the desired effect

62. I have sometimes found myself manipulating my partner into having sex

63. Sex is something that shouldn't be talked about a great deal

64. Inhibitions are not necessary in sex as long as both partners are comfortable and there is nothing done that is morally wrong

65. I find I have sex more for my own enjoyment rather than for the sake of my partner

66. I usually have to go through a set ritual to enjoy sex

67. I always have to have some sort of control over what is happening when having sex

68. Lack of education and sex skills can have a negative impact on one's sex life

69. There is no such thing as a nymphomaniac

70. I think it is important to be satisfied sexually early in your relationship because you never know for how long you will have a good sex life

71. A man is responsible for pleasing a woman and a woman is responsible for pleasing a man

72. Other than tension release, there is a lack of pleasure during or following sex

73. I feel guilty when I think about memories of my sex life

74. It is important to know everything about how one responds sexually

75. I would nearly always rather do something I love than have sex

76. My sexual needs are never going to be met if I have to depend upon someone else

77. I would not rate my sexual desire as being low

78. You have to be careful because the more you learn about sex the more complicated you can make it

79. Woman's bodies are more about having children than enjoying sex

80. I think most old people don't have a good sex life

81. When I tell my partner what I would like them to do during sex I find the mood gets lost

82. I can't stand missing out on sex

83. I would never find it difficult to let my partner bathe me

84. I hardly ever fantasise about having sex with my partner

85. I never think my partner enjoys sex far more than I do

86. I would never resent my partner for refusing my sexual advances

87. My sexual pleasure is over with very quickly when I make love

88. Sex education is not necessary to have lifelong fulfilment sexually

89. Most women only have sex to please their men, rather than to please themselves

90. Complications with one's sex life tend to get worse over the years

91. I'd rather have input in deciding what we are going to do sexually instead of what my partner thinks best at the time

92. When I know my partner isn't interested I never push for sex

93. I never feel inhibited about having sex with my partner

94. It is natural to be sexually curious

95. I never wonder what all the fuss is about sex

96. Sometimes my sex life gets out of control

97. I'm what you would call a screamer when I climax

98. Sex is not a simple, uncomplicated process

99. Sex is just as satisfying for a woman as it is for a man

100. The longer a relationship goes on the harder it is to find time for sex

SEXUAL BELIEFS SCORE SHEET

1 ___ Agree Disagree *
2 ___ Agree Disagree *
3 ___ Agree Disagree *
4 ___ Agree Disagree **
5 ___ Agree Disagree **
6 ___ Agree Disagree *
7 ___ Agree Disagree *
8 ___ Agree Disagree *
9 ___ Agree Disagree *
10 ___ Agree Disagree *
11 ___ Agree Disagree **
12 ___ Agree Disagree **

13 ___ Agree Disagree *
14 ___ Agree Disagree **
15 ___ Agree Disagree **
16 ___ Agree Disagree **
17 ___ Agree Disagree **
18 ___ Agree Disagree *
19 ___ Agree Disagree *
20 ___ Agree Disagree **
21 ___ Agree Disagree *
22 ___ Agree Disagree **
23 ___ Agree Disagree *
24 ___ Agree Disagree *
25 ___ Agree Disagree **
26 ___ Agree Disagree *
27 ___ Agree Disagree *
28 ___ Agree Disagree *
29 ___ Agree Disagree **
30 ___ Agree Disagree **
31 ___ Agree Disagree **
32 ___ Agree Disagree **
33 ___ Agree Disagree *
34 ___ Agree Disagree *
35 ___ Agree Disagree **
36 ___ Agree Disagree **
37 ___ Agree Disagree **
38 ___ Agree Disagree *
39 ___ Agree Disagree **
40 ___ Agree Disagree **
41 ___ Agree Disagree **
42 ___ Agree Disagree *
43 ___ Agree Disagree **
44 ___ Agree Disagree **
45 ___ Agree Disagree **
46 ___ Agree Disagree *

47 ___ Agree Disagree *
48 ___ Agree Disagree **
49 ___ Agree Disagree *
50 ___ Agree Disagree *
51 ___ Agree Disagree *
52 ___ Agree Disagree **
53 ___ Agree Disagree *
54 ___ Agree Disagree **
55 ___ Agree Disagree *
56 ___ Agree Disagree **
57 ___ Agree Disagree **
58 ___ Agree Disagree **
59 ___ Agree Disagree **
60 ___ Agree Disagree **
61 ___ Agree Disagree **
62 ___ Agree Disagree *
63 ___ Agree Disagree *
64 ___ Agree Disagree **
65 ___ Agree Disagree **
66 ___ Agree Disagree *
67 ___ Agree Disagree *
68 ___ Agree Disagree **
69 ___ Agree Disagree *
70 ___ Agree Disagree *
71 ___ Agree Disagree *
72 ___ Agree Disagree *
73 ___ Agree Disagree *
74 ___ Agree Disagree **
75 ___ Agree Disagree *
76 ___ Agree Disagree *
77 ___ Agree Disagree **
78 ___ Agree Disagree *
79 ___ Agree Disagree *
80 ___ Agree Disagree *

81 ___ Agree Disagree *
82 ___ Agree Disagree *
83 ___ Agree Disagree **
84 ___ Agree Disagree *
85 ___ Agree Disagree **
86 ___ Agree Disagree **
87 ___ Agree Disagree *
88 ___ Agree Disagree **
89 ___ Agree Disagree *
90 ___ Agree Disagree *
91 ___ Agree Disagree **
92 ___ Agree Disagree **
93 ___ Agree Disagree **
94 ___ Agree Disagree **
95 ___ Agree Disagree **
96 ___ Agree Disagree *
97 ___ Agree Disagree **
98 ___ Agree Disagree **
99 ___ Agree Disagree **
100 __ Agree Disagree *[23]

TOTAL SCORES

1 ___
2 ___
3 ___
4 ___
5 ___
6 ___
7 ___
8 ___
9 ___
0 ___

SCORING THE SEXUAL BELIEFS INVENTORY

STEP ONE

Single – asterisk items

* If the item has one asterisk and you circle the word "Agree", give your self one point in the place provided

Double-asterisk items

** If the item has two asterisks and you circled the word "Disagree", give yourself a point in the place provided

STEP TWO

Tally your points

Add up all the items 1, 11, 21, 31, 41, 51, 61, 71, 81, 91 and enter the total under the total scores section at the bottom next to the number 1. The higher the number of points the greater your agreement with the irrational idea that - **A man is responsible for pleasing a woman and a woman is responsible for pleasing a man**

Communicating what we like and dislike about sex is important. If we don't communicate we are expecting our partner to read our mind to know what has the best effect. Furthermore, we are more likely to hold them responsible for our sexual frustration or lack of pleasure. We need to understand that we have to take the responsibility for our own pleasure by communicating our preferences, what feels good and what doesn't. Only then can our partner be tuned to our individual and unique preferences so that he or she can grow in expertise in pleasing us.

Add up all the items 2, 12, 22, 32, 42, 52, 62, 72, 82, 92 and enter the total under the total scores section at the bottom next to number 2.
The higher the number of points the greater your agreement with the irrational idea that - **Compulsive sex is okay**

Unfortunately many relationships suffer from compulsive sex. It is the fixation on sexual release to the exclusion of love, respect, mutuality, one's partner's needs and total relationship commitment. It is a selfish one-sided approach which in reality views the act as more important than the partner. It is di-

vorced of love and its only focus is sexual release for the initiator. It stifles the spiritual, romantic, emotional, relational components of the relationship.

Add up all the items 3, 13, 23, 33, 43, 53, 63, 73, 83, 93 and enter the total down under the total scores section at the bottom next to number 3.
The higher the number of points the greater your agreement with the irrational idea that - **Sex is dirty or wrong (or there has been an experience of guilt associated with it)**
One of the major inhibitions to an enjoyable sex life is the false belief that sex is wrong, dirty, embarrassing, shameful and shouldn't be enjoyable. Sometimes this occurs when people have had previously bad sexual experiences, or those that have produced guilt or false guilt. Being comfortable with one's own body is also important before one can be comfortable while being naked with their partner. It is especially important for women to be guilt free in their sexuality in order that they can give themselves permission to enjoy the sexual experience. Without this giving permission, many women hinder their sexual feelings. We need to understand that we are designed to be sexual and designed for pleasure. If we hold back for "religious reasons" to inhibit our sexuality we only promote the myth that enjoyment of sexuality is evil rather than good.

Add up all the items 4, 14, 24, 34, 44, 54, 64, 74, 84, 94 and enter the total down under the total scores section at the bottom next to the number 4.
The higher the number of points the greater your agreement with the irrational idea that - **Sexual curiosity is not natural and sexual responsiveness is not innate**
This erroneous idea leads people to seek sexual fulfilment through learning skills rather than tapping into their innate responsiveness to sex. Thinking that sexual curiosity is wrong or not natural leads people to inhibit their sexual desires and responses. Sexual responses are activated by the parasympa-

thetic nervous system; this means you have to be relaxed for them to work properly. Anxiety is foreign to a great sex life. A woman lubricates vaginally every 80-90 minutes while she sleeps just as a man gets an erection every 80-90 minutes while he sleeps.

Add up all the items 5, 15, 25, 35, 45, 55, 65, 75, 85, 95 and enter the total under the total scores section at the bottom next to the number 5. The higher the number of points the greater your agreement with the irrational idea that - **Sex is not that important (hypo sexual desire disorder/abuse association)**

Sex is the one aspect that sets apart marriage and intimate relationships from every other relationship. To take away the sexual component from our intimate relationship turns our relationship into that of housemates. To deny our sexuality in our intimate relationship often says more about the health of our relationship outside the bedroom because sex often mirrors the relationship. The myth of sex being not that important is often more indicative of the negative experiences of sexuality that we might have had or our own inability to connect with our sexuality.

Add up all the items 6, 16, 26, 36, 46, 56, 66, 76, 86, 96 and enter the total under the total scores section at the bottom next to the number 6. The higher the number of points the greater your agreement with the irrational idea that - **Love means sex; if a person rejects you they don't love you (Sexual addiction)**

Many men connect sex with love. This leads one to think that rejection of sexual advances equates to loss of love. This can be destructive to relationships because of the resentments that result due to rejection of sexual advances. Sexual addiction occurs when a person feels controlled by the urge and believes that sex is their most important need. Sexual addicts often indulge in sabotaging their relationships with their spouse in order to justify seeking their sexual needs being met in their addiction. For example, fighting with their spouse in order to rationalise their entitlement to seek sexual release with pornography.

Add up all the items 7, 17, 27, 37, 47, 57, 67, 77, 87, 97 and enter the total under the total scores section at the bottom next to the number 7. The higher the number of points the greater your agreement with the irrational idea that - **Sex is really only for men and it is not lady-like for women to completely enjoy it**

Women inhibit their arousal level and climaxes by inhibiting the physiological responses. Women may need to remove a block which is robbing them of sexual enjoyment. It might be reducing fear, building trust with their partner or simply giving themselves permission to connect with their sexuality and say it is okay to be a sexual person. This false belief is one of the main reasons why some women never feel the intensity of climax that is available to them. To change this, a woman needs to give herself permission to enjoy sex or may need to undo any rigid, anti-sex teaching she has learnt.

Add up all the items 8, 18, 28, 38, 48, 58, 68, 78, 88, 98 and enter the total under the total scores section at the bottom next to the number 8. The higher the number of points the greater your agreement with the irrational idea that - **Sex works perfectly if you just do what comes naturally (afraid of sex education)**

Sex education can remove blocks which currently inhibit you or your partner's natural responsiveness. We tend to stimulate our partners the way in which we want to be stimulated; that is, men stimulate women the way men want to be stimulated. Understanding the different gender needs for example can dramatically improve our sex lives just as understanding how to be a skilful lover can enhance pleasure. Some people are afraid of sex education, others are too proud to allow themselves to think that they can be taught anything new in this area, while others are threatened by any changes to their sexual formats.

Add up all the items 9, 19, 29, 39, 49, 59, 69, 79, 89, 99 and enter the total under the total scores section at the bottom next to the number 9. The higher the number of points the greater your agreement with the irrational idea that - **Women are not as sexual as men**

This belief, even if only one partner believes it, is very destructive to relationships. While women can be derailed easily through the refusal of their partner to meet their emotional needs which are generally a prerequisite for women's long term sexual enjoyment, when these needs are met and a woman gives herself permission for enjoyment, many women unleash a growing desire for sexual satisfaction. It is after all, the woman who has the only feature that has been created to serve exclusively as a sexual pleasure organ, and have the ability to produce repeated climaxes in a singular, sexual experience. Unfortunately, it is often previous negative experiences that builds aversion to sexuality in women, and shuts down their natural responsiveness.

Add up all the items 10, 20, 30, 40, 50, 60, 70, 80, 90, 100 and enter the total under the total scores section at the bottom next to the number 0. The higher the number of points the greater your agreement with the irrational idea that - **Sex deteriorates in long term relationships (or with age)**

When we have this belief it tends to become a self-fulfilling prophecy – we start to look for the evidence to prove our belief and we always find evidence for what we believe. Sex deteriorates in relationships often because it has been moved down the list of priorities, or blocks have been perpetuated that turned down responsiveness. Sex can actually improve with age if a couple accurately communicate their likes and dislikes, if they are accepting and accommodating of their partner's differences and if their relationship outside the bedroom is growing positively as well. With age certain anxieties are removed, such as fear of pregnancy or fear of not being understood.

End of Inventory

So what score is significant in the above inventory? If you have three or more then there could be an irrational belief in the corresponding area that needs dealing with. The number three might only be marginal but if you had a score greater than five in any area then you might have discovered something quite significant which, when addressed could result in a very positive change to your sexuality and pleasure.

SUMMARY OF CHAPTER EIGHT

A. Back at the beginning

1. Life was simple, but now we are busy with complex structures and routines. You must -
a) Change the things you can.
b) Keep your life in balance.
c) Reduce the killers and increase the aphrodisiacs.
d) Keep healthy.
e) Learn to relax.
f) Keep a positive attitude.
g) Accept the bad times and restrict their impact.
h) Use no unnatural crutches.

2. Early love provides energy.
a) Plan to regain the energy romance provides.
b) Be prepared to push yourself for romance.

3. It used to be top priority. Be thrifty with time to put romance higher on your list of priorities.

4. Both partners used to look their best. Pay attention to appearance again.

5. Increase sharing, connecting and bonding with your spouse as

you used to early in the relationship.

6. Decrease the negatives and concentrate on your partner's positives, especially in the bedroom. Be aware of the power of mind sex.

7. Help your man learn the art of making love to your mind first.

8. Introduce more sexual play outside the bedroom.

9. Emphasise passion again.

10. Introduce fun, frolic and play again.

11. Substitute predictability with spontaneity and variety. Teach your man the importance of preparing you for lovemaking.

12. Educate your man on the importance of the female erection.

B. The primary male fantasy is a woman crazy with desire for her man.
>Show desire for your man without rejection.
>Be more aggressive and initiate lovemaking.

C. Both partners need to be educated concerning what turns the other on.

D. Consider increasing *shared* pleasure time during lovemaking.

E. Communicate your likes and dislikes clearly. Consider the indicator and accelerator technique.

F. The little things count. Consider swapping romantic vouchers.

G. Explore you and your partner's sexual beliefs to eradicate irrational beliefs that might be holding you back.

CHAPTER NINE

TEN THINGS THAT BLOCK ROMANCE

"Her heart was wild, but I didn't want to catch it, I wanted to run with it, to set mine free." (Atticus)

Sometimes you can be spending a great deal of effort, and be doing all the right things, but your man still seems to be a long way from being a romantic. This chapter deals with areas that can block romance in your man and will also show you how to remove those blocks.

1. Criticism

How much do you criticise your man? The amount could well indicate the size of the block you are placing in the path of him becoming a romantic. Sometimes we can fall into the habit of criticising our partner because we are frustrated in some other area of our relationship. We can make ourselves feel so strongly about certain issues when so often the criticisms can be in areas that are really of little consequence.

Criticism does not provide a strong motivation for change. In fact, it often makes the person resent it, act passive aggressive or merely produce a superficial, short-term change. A better motivation for change is a positive, affirming approach. Think about it. Who would you be more likely to change for - a person you love, admire and know that they think you are the greatest and are always telling you so, or a critical person who dislikes you and who is always telling you off? The answer is clear and yet so many people still try to change their partners by continual criticism. After ten years of nagging you would think they would change their tactics, but no, once the habit of criticism has been laid it is very difficult to break. Criticism can open your whole relationship to a negative tone and generate lethargy on behalf of both partners towards their relationship.

> *Criticism does not provide a strong motivation for change.*

Make a careful appraisal of your attitude and ask your closest friends where they would score you on the criticiser/encourager scale. If you or your friends score you high on the criticism side you will have to change your approach drastically if you wish your spouse to be romantic. Nothing kills romance as quick or for as long as criticism. When you think or read of a romantic couple in a romantic setting doing romantic things you cannot imagine criticism dominating the atmosphere. In fact, it's just the opposite. Romance usually has both partners affirming each other, complimenting each other, and drawing attention to the other's strengths.

Warren Farrell gives the advice to make sure that your compliments outpace your criticism by four to one, any less and you need help![24] By affirming your man you are bonding him to you, meeting his needs, making him feel happy with himself, as well as nurturing his self-esteem. Such a contented man is far more able to meet his partner's needs, and indeed far more likely to **want** to meet those needs. Furthermore, if you connect the affirmation with his romantic attempts, in a genuine and non-patronising way, then he will feel good about being a romantic.

Two of our most basic needs as humans are to love but also to be loved. To be appreciated is to be loved in a special way. By affirming and admiring your man you will bind him to you closer than anyone else. Criticism does the opposite; it erects blocks to closeness and intimacy.

What areas can you appreciate in your spouse? Any area that relates to him *as a man* is important. Also, his talents and abilities, his individuality, his work, his personality, his temperament, and what *he thinks* he is best at. A man's self-esteem is strongly related to his work and although other people may congratulate him on his efforts at work, even his colleagues or superiors' commendations are not on the same par as his spouse's admiration and appreciation. Many men also thrive on admiration of their physical attributes. A young bride told of "how much her husband hated to care for the yard, but after admiring his muscles when he was mowing the lawn, she had no more problem".[25] By eliminating unnecessary criticism, adding admiration to essential criticism, and just increasing the daily amount of affirmation and appreciation towards your man, you can remove barriers to intimacy and lay the foundation for romance. Expressions of love ignite love in return, so that the appreciative woman finds her man bonded to her, loving her in return, happy in himself and happy to respond.

Sometimes criticism will be used in a sub conscious attempt to draw a man closer to a woman. The trouble is that it usually has the opposite effect. It is the wrong tool to use to manipulate a man. Criticism is used sometimes because it provokes a response, some communication or a verbal commitment to change. In so many relationships it is the woman who is continually reaching for her man, wanting him to take the initiative and spend quality time with her. But he never does take the initiative and so she thinks she can rectify the problem by criticism, manipulation, threats, using sex as a weapon or as a bargaining tool. Or she challenges any activity that she feels he may be giving more attention to than her, or some activity that she *interprets* as giving him more enjoyment than her. Does it motivate him to change? No. Does this endear her to him? No, in fact it drives him from her faster than anything else does. I have seen this issue played out countless times in so many couples. It seems people often live with it for years treating it as an impasse. Often the couple themselves don't even understand what is happening. So what is going on here and what can be done about it?

The amount of criticism and controlling is often in direct proportion to the lack of quality time the woman *feels* she is missing out on. The key words are *"Quality time"* and *"feels,"*. If there are extenuating circumstances or because of family or work commitments, a woman can put on hold her need to feel close to her man. But she can only do this for a limited time. If she doesn't "feel" needed, loved and appreciated she can rebel and become critical or controlling. It is not the amount of quality time that is important, rather it is whether **she feels** her man wants to be with her and gives her his full, devoted, undivided attention (like he used to) because she is special to him. This is what satisfies her, this and this alone. Criticism, manipulation and even fits of rage just do not work because the initiation to spend quality time must come from the man.

> *The amount of criticism and controlling is often in direct proportion to the lack of quality time the woman FEELS she is missing out on.*

The solution is for the couple to work out a commitment to "super quality time". This is time spent where the couple sit down and share where they are at in their relationship, their hurts, their feelings and their commitment to each other. Once a man can truly dedicate himself to this "super quality time," the woman doesn't feel she has to compete for his attention. She learns to relax and loses her intensity for reaching at him constantly, because she knows he does in fact love her, he is satisfying her needs and she is able to allow him freedom instead of pulling him to her. She now *feels* loved.

2. Anger

How you handle anger in your relationship can be a stumbling block or a stepping stone to romance. It is important that anger is expressed, but within acceptable guidelines, because if it isn't expressed it only builds. Accumulated anger kills love and the partner has no clue to the unexpressed anger or is bewildered at the one straw that has broken the camel's back.

The wrong expression of anger can be the result of faulty communication. Where a couple have excellent communication, anger can be accepted and tolerated because there is a proper understanding of both the partner and the cause of the anger. When there is good communication our spouse can see the world through our eyes and can become part of the solution rather than part of the anger. Good communication also helps our partner to see our anger as being separate from the person. To merge the anger and the person means that if they can't handle the anger then they can't handle the person as well. It is far better if both partners can see anger as being event related rather than person related. We can still love the person even though the event they may have been involved in caused us anger. Learn to get angry at events, behaviours or things, don't personalise anger so that you blame the person involved, especially when it's your spouse. This doesn't mean that the person ultimately responsible for the behaviour is allowed to get off Scot free. What it means is that you can preserve the pathways of communication so that it can be worked out, resolved and the person can understand how or why he hurt you, without trying to justify or excuse his actions.

> *When there is good communication our spouse can see the world through our eyes and can become part of the solution rather than part of the anger.*

If you find you are becoming angry over small things consistently, you need to find the root cause of your frustration. Some women at times allow anger to become a signal of frustration without realising it, or feel helpless to resolve the underlying cause of anger in their relationship. In such cases, such a person may need professional help to pinpoint the underlying cause. Sometimes the underlying cause is of a physiological nature, such as hormone imbalances, which can occur especially at menopause, but can occur at other times as well. The point is that there can be simple, medical solutions to physiological problems rather than intensive psychological counselling.

Make sure you can overcome your anger quickly rather than brooding over it for long periods of time. Adopt a positive approach to life and try to not take your anger out on the innocent ones in your life. When your man gets angry, learn to soothe him by listening, whether or not you or someone else is the target for his anger. When we become the objects of anger, or feel angry ourselves, withdrawal is often the result. Sometimes the intensity of anger can be lessened through touch with our partner. At other times a man may just need a little space to deal with his emotions. If his partner can insulate herself at these times so that she does not take anything personally, she will be able to diffuse the anger and soothe her man. Unfortunately many a woman will want to involve herself in her man's emotions so much that when a man is feeling angry and wishes to withdraw a woman will press and crowd her man and only compound his problem. If she could learn to just give him a little space at that time she would find he would be more likely to talk about it at other times. Anger can be diffused when it is accepted, validated, understood and soothed by our partner. It can be released naturally when dealt with in the right way but if it is left to accumulate and continue to annoy, it can rob us of our health or our relationship to others, as we lash out at those who are not responsible for the anger. If you are angry in one area in your life, don't let it have the effect of harming all the other areas as well. Limit it to its own area and decide that nothing will rob you of the beauty to be gained in other areas of your relationship or life.

3. Past Conflicts

The problem with past conflicts is that they often don't remain in the past but interrupt the present and threaten the future. There may be issues in your relationship in the past for which your mate has apologised. He may be truly sorry for the hurt he has caused but for some reason or another it never gets completely forgiven, or at least never forgotten. I know of one woman who has never forgiven her partner for picking up a men's magazine. It was a spare of the moment decision and was hidden but found by the wife. The point is that the wife during any subsequent conflict has raised this issue for the past twenty years. The result is that conflicts are not resolved but it is left to one partner to either withdraw, yield or lose. Now, unfortunately, the whole relationship is viewed with insecurity and suspicion on behalf of the wife because the past has not been dealt with sufficiently. The trouble is that the longer a wound remains unhealed, the harder it is to deal with. In this particular case the wife finds it hard to forgive and forget because she finds it a type of trump card in any argument between her and her spouse, which instantly earns her bonus points. The problem however, is that any of these totally unrelated conflicts remain unresolved and the original hurt becomes relived and compounded.

The key to stop past conflicts from becoming blocks to romance is to forgive and forget. We may say we forgive, and may even believe so ourselves, but our actions will give us away. For some reason we often want to hold on to past grievances, whether to use as a wedge, or just to console us as to how our partner must be wrong this time because he was wrong on the past occasion. The problem for our partner however, is that the past can't be changed and no amount of future behaviour can change the past. It is a no win situation for him. No matter what he does, he cannot change the past, even if he remains indebted to you for life. Unfortunately, this is one of the reasons why we often do not want to let go of the upper hand in our relationship. We like the idea of our spouse being indebted to us for life as it keeps the power balance in our favour.

When we analyse the results for relationships where past wrongs are not forgiven, we find that instead of being an advantage to one partner, they become detrimental to both. But it doesn't stop there. Children have a sensitive radar for conflict between mum and dad. To grow up in a home full of conflict can be one of the worst gifts parents can give their children. Not only does unforgiveness leave issues unresolved, compounds frustration and sets a hostile tone to the relationship, but it also encourages our spouse to look for our faults and short comings and to not forgive us. The fact is that no amount of our making mileage out of past wrongs is going to improve our relationship *now*. Not forgiving a past wrong will only allow the wrong to have more power over us and rob us of the beauty our relationship has to offer us now and in the future. The power of the past wrong can be short-circuited by the wronged partner, by forgiving totally, forgetting and not allowing it to surface again. In this way you refuse to let it affect the relationship both now and in the future. So you see although the partner who wrongs is the person who cannot change the past, it is the person who is wronged who is the one who can determine whether it effects the future.

> *Not forgiving a past wrong will only allow the wrong to have more power over us and rob us of the beauty our relationship has to offer us now and in the future.*

What we must all do is be prepared to start a clean sheet in our relationship. No more hanging on to past wrongs or letting them have any power in determining the quality of our relationship. It is true that you have far more to lose by holding on to past wrongs than by forgiving them. Forgiving the past is better for your health as well as your relationship. You will never lose by forgiving someone. Forgiveness is not a licence to do it again but an enabling power to heal wounds and build the future of your relationship.

Once you have decided you need to let go of a particular past wrong committed by your spouse, seal it by talking to him about it. Ask his forgiveness for not forgiving him completely earlier and ask for his help to forget it in the future. You may find the floodgates of romance open like never before.

4. Inability To Resolve Conflict

Another barrier to romance can be resolving conflicts in negative ways. This simply means that there are right ways and wrong ways to fight. We have already mentioned the negative impact that bringing up past conflicts has on a relationship. We have also looked at anger and criticism but another factor is the power balance in your relationship. Many couples live very satisfied lives with the power balance just marginally favouring one or the other. But problems occur when the power goes to the extreme. An excessively weighted power balance in favour of one partner can be just as destructive to a relationship as any other block. Where a man has an excessive power balance favouring him in the relationship, the woman becomes submissive, dominated, frustrated, depressed and loses her own individuality, especially in her man's presence. Where there is an excessive power balance in favour of the woman, this too has its problems. The woman may want to dictate romance (which doesn't work) and therefore she can lose respect for her man by his continued submission without protest.

What can be done to even the power balance? This can be very difficult as the person with the upper hand is usually very insecure and does not wish to relinquish control. They have to find security in a loving, balanced relationship and learn to let go. They have to experience the freedom of unselfishness and the joy of seeing their partner's individuality. On the other hand, the dominated partner needs to build their self-esteem, have confidence in their own decisions and establish their own individuality for the benefit of both the relationship and themselves. They need to insist on their own needs being met in addition to their partner's needs being met. They need to explain to their partner that their relationship must be based on love, and if it is not based on love then they have nothing. Love never seeks to dominate or enslave, rather it draws through sharing.

> *Love never seeks to dominate or enslave, rather it draws through sharing.*

Someone has once said. "If you want to test a man's character, give him power." In intimate relationships there is ample opportunity for manipulation and the abuse of power, by either partner. But something that must be preserved is the free will of the other. Sometimes the power balance can be even but we will still try and control our mate. It may only be in little things yet we may still try and boss or coerce our mate for the very sake of control. The best romantic advice I gave to one couple was to stop bossing your mate. Does it really matter so much if your partner wishes to do something his or her way? Freedom to do something our way in little things, even if it takes longer, has to be preserved. A man has absolutely no motivation to become romantic if his partner bosses him. Allow your man freedom where ever possible and you will find him contented and much more accepting of romance.

Some men have had the wrong role model of resolving conflict. They may not be bossed, or have an unequal power balance but conflict will still lead to frustration because it is not resolved. One man related how he learned from his father the role model of how to deal with conflict. Whenever his parents started fighting and if it could not be resolved quickly, the father would take his wife by the hand and lead her to the bedroom. There he would lock the door, thus barring the children. As a child the man can remember wondering whatever happened behind closed doors - how they sorted things out. The role model men get from their fathers resolving conflict can be quite important. Imagine the resentment from the wife at her husband's insistence on sex when she was ready to fight. Imagine too how the issues would never have been dealt with properly.

It is often because a man does not know how to express his feelings that his sexuality becomes the medium for all of his feelings.[26] Men are tuned to the physical world, and it is in the physical act of sex that they can often express lots of their emotions. The trouble is when a man uses sex to express his negative emotions, sex can become negative as well. If a man is angry, upset, disappointed or grieved, his sexuality can reflect it by becoming aggressive, rough, one sided or even disinterested in sex altogether. This is when a man needs to be encouraged to express his feelings verbally so that only love, tenderness, mutual satisfaction and enjoyment are reserved for sex.

> *It is often because a man does not know how to express his feelings that his sexuality becomes the medium for all of his feelings.*

If sex is used as the only method for settling disputes, then sex becomes negative instead of positive. Encourage your man to express his feelings verbally and reserve sex for making up after arguments when it can be positive and bonding.

It is really beyond the scope of this book to highlight all of the principles of conflict resolution. Indeed, there are whole books that deal with that topic alone. If arguments are not resolved quickly but linger on for days and days then you may need extra help. The important point is for you both to see the issue at stake rather than personalising it and attacking the person rather than the point of view. This way you can still disagree but not let it affect your personal lives, including your sex lives. Make sure you both get the facts correct to begin with and don't jump to conclusions. Develop an attitude of admitting when you are wrong and agree to not argue in public. Make arguments a time of growth and understanding without the love for your partner diminishing. Resolving conflict in a positive way by reaching an agreement without either partner losing face will add stability to your relationship. It will mean that romance will never be threatened by a conflict in any area of your relationship.

5. Sarcasm

Sarcasm in any form can be cutting and can rob any area of its power or pleasure. When it comes to romance, sarcasm is often used to discredit romance quickly before the "discreditor" has to deal with the responsibility of taking it seriously. For the woman who wants her man to be a romantic, she must be prepared to handle sarcasm before its destructive effects are allowed to ridicule romance. Sarcasm basically comes from three sources - others, your man and yourself. Let's have a closer look at these three areas and see how we can deal with each of them.

How To Stop Sarcasm At Romance And Intimacy.
1. Sarcasm From Others

Some men who wish to get on with their peers and at the same time like to see themselves as macho, will often use sarcasm when in a group. Their favourite ploy will be to start a war between the sexes by drawing attention to a so-called weakness in women and show the corresponding strength in men. The other approach is to attack long term intimate relationships such as marriage in general, by the use of jokes. Sometimes, if ignored, these men will eventually go onto another topic and little harm can be done. But sometimes a man may have a dig at your man's specific romantic gestures such as him buying you flowers or a card. Instead of your man losing face you can turn it around to his advantage by affirming your man. You can say how he is not ignorant of how to turn a woman on because he can be romantic if he wants to be (this still gives him the control in front of his friends). Explain how other women would really envy you if they knew his romantic skills. You can say that you both don't see it as mushy because your relationship is so much better off with romance.

By taking this approach you have appealed to areas which men respect, that is, a good lover, power (over women and to choose for themselves) and secret knowledge that they are missing out on. Furthermore, you have reinforced romance in your man and you have not tried to start a fight by directly attacking the originator of the sarcastic comments. You will find that the emphasis will possibly shift from attacks on your man's romantic nature to jibes about what a Casanova he is, all in keeping with the spirit of humour. If you can learn to laugh at yourself and turn it back on the originator, rather than take such sarcasm as a personal attack, you will develop a good defence and the problem will be short lived and not a problem at all.

2. Sarcasm From Your Man.

The best way to handle sarcasm from your partner is to remind him of the strengths of romance. For instance, if he thinks some romantic behaviour to be too silly or sissy, you can say, "But you didn't think last Wednesday night was too silly or sissy when after that night out you enjoyed making love." Or, "I was so turned on because you were such a romantic." What man could argue with such a response? You could further respond by saying how if your man didn't want so much enjoyment in bed, or didn't want you to have so much enjoyment in bed, then maybe romance should be curbed, but you know that he doesn't want such enjoyment to cease. Any man who has a normal, healthy sex drive will quickly quit while he is miles ahead.

3. Sarcasm From Yourself.

You may be surprised that I have included sarcasm from yourself. Although not overtly sarcastic against romance you could be guilty of acting in a manner that will have the same results as sarcasm. Sometimes women do not know how to accept romantic gestures from their spouses in public and will treat it the same as they do a compliment by playing down its importance or effect. Some women, with a low self-image will think they are not worthy of a compliment and will say the compliment is not true. The point is that a "romantic play down" is the counterpart of romantic sarcasm.

> *A "romantic play down" is the counterpart of romantic sarcasm.*

If you play down a romantic gesture or comment from your partner, especially in public, you are only encouraging him to be unromantic. Make sure you can accept his romantic gestures and respond without becoming embarrassed, questioning his genuineness or acting as if you do not like his romantic attempts. Always accept his attempts as genuine rather than responding with sarcasm. Do not play down but accept and enhance all of his romantic efforts by encouraging him to continue. Accept his attempts with delight, do not send mixed messages that will confuse. In this way you will encourage him to be more romantic both privately and publicly.

6. Depression

No one is exempt from feeling depressed at one stage or another during their lives. But some people seem to have more than their fair share. Depression can be a block to romance especially when it is lasting or when men do not know how to react to it.

Sometimes depression can be cause related. That is, there is a cause for the depression that is clearly evident. It could be failure, dashed hopes, tragedy, accidental or interpersonal. But for a lot of times when people get depressed there is not always a clearly evident cause. They do not know why they are depressed, they just know they are depressed. Some psychologists can pinpoint past experiences in our lives that are at the centre of our depression, other times it can be a physiologically related problem.

When you think about the general down feelings of depression with the lack of motivation for anything, you can see how blatantly it contrasts with romance. In fact some characteristics are actually the very opposite to romance. Remember reading the chapter on the characteristics of romance where we discussed how romance provides energy and motivation. It is positive and instils hope. Romance looks on the positive, "love is blind" side, whereas depression only looks at the negative and is blind to the positive things. So the two cannot live together, they are just so opposite. The good part is that if you have a happy, romantic relationship with your spouse, it can be hard for your depression to last - it is forced out by the romance in your life. But how do you keep the motivation for romance when you get depressed? Here are a few suggestions that should help.

1. Keep your life in balance. Keep your priorities in order and add pleasant tasks to arduous ones.

2. Provide goals. We all need goals in life. Make sure you have attainable short and long term goals. By fixing our attention on the goal it makes the workload easier to bear.

3. Provide breaks. Holidays are important to keep balance. Times of recreation are important to stop burnout and discontentment.

4. Develop creative interests. Have you ever wanted to learn a musical instrument, or develop a talent or skill but never had the time or opportunity? Surely you can afford at least an hour or so each week in which to do so.

5. Keep your body healthy. Junk food feeds depression and so too does lack of exercise. Develop a regular exercise program that you enjoy and discipline yourself to stick to it at all costs. The secret is to find a program that you enjoy so that you find it easy to stick to and so it does not become another chore to add to the list each day. Eat a nutritious diet with plenty of fresh fruit and vegetables and let nature automatically fight any depression for you.

6. Care for your appearance. If you look good, you can feel good. A few dollars spent on caring for your hair and appearance is worth hundreds in dividends.

7. Organise yourself. It may be that you have procrastinated on those unwanted tasks that is really getting you down. Work out a strategy and a time program of how and when they will get done.

8. Live life in peace with as many as possible. Peace can provide motivation to live a happy balanced life, whereas guilt or anger can cause depression and turmoil. Make right past offences where you can and learn to get on with every one as much as possible.

9. Cultivate friendship and friendliness. The person who has a lot of close, true friends has a powerful weapon against depression. Do not sour friendships by using friends but be eager to help them.

10. Keep yourself busy. Busy people find it hard to stay depressed for long - they just do not have the time. Conversely, bored people slip into depression far more easily.

11. Help others. Making a positive contribution by helping those in need provides an outside focus. When we focus only on ourselves and our own needs, it is easier to become egocentric and depressed.

12. Talk about your depression. Do not deny your depression but get it out where you can deal with it. Talking to your close friends can help release it and look for positive aids and ways of dealing with it.

13. Explore your spiritual dimension. In such a physically dominated world we can forget our spiritual needs. Develop your spiritual nature and inject those spiritual virtues of love, peace, happiness, contentment, acceptance and hope into your physical being.

14. Become needed. Many people become depressed because they think they have no reason to live, they are not wanted by anyone, or their own needs are not met. By becoming an active, participatory family member one can see they are needed and wanted by others. Children are not independent, they need others to care for them. By putting time and effort into family life one can feel needed. When children leave home, sometimes by having a close contributory role in another family, a woman can fill this void in her life in small doses making it much more manageable.

7. Lethargy and Apathy

Although similar to depression, lethargy and apathy usually have an attitude problem at their base. Have you ever wanted to stay home because you just cannot be bothered with the effort it takes to go out, while on the other hand your partner is rearing to go out and rage? Usually the effort is overestimated when we are lethargic and the answer can often be in a review of our priorities. If you constantly feel you have no energy it is best to see your doctor. But a lot of the time it is because romance gets pushed down on our list of priorities and our energy is consumed with those higher up the order. A person can often have his or her lethargy and apathy cured instantly, given the right motivation. Take a night when your lover comes home and it is cold and wet. He suggests you go out for dinner but you just cannot bear the thought of leaving the heater. Twenty minutes later the phone rings and a motor vehicle dealer tells you, "You have won a brand new car, can you come down and pick it up right away?" Or your child had an accident at a friend's place, "Can you come over and accompany them to hospital for treatment?" All of a sudden the bonds that tied you to that heater that seemed to be as strong as chains, are now like paper. There is no thought about a decision of whether to go or stay, no hesitation, you just go.

> *A person can often have his or her lethargy and apathy cured instantly, given the right motivation.*

You could have waited until tomorrow to pick up a new car but no, most people would do it as soon as they could. Some things motivate us whereas others could never get us to budge an inch, and it's all to do with what motivates us, our priorities and attitude. Sometimes it's good to look at ourselves and analyse our enthusiasm for life. What sort of atmosphere do I create where I go? Is it one of enthusiasm or apathy? Whichever it is, it can be changed by our attitude. We can decide whether we are going to have a zest for living, for going out, for doing romantic things or not.

At times our energy is so absorbed by all the necessary duties of life, home, work and motherhood that we just can't seem to get the necessary motivation for the "extras". The problem is that when life goes on like this for months or years then energy levels are not replenished and what was once a joy becomes a task. The "extras" are there to make the necessities bearable, and to replenish our energy and zest to cope with the necessities. If we have no enthusiasm for the "extras", the romantic niceties, why are we where we are, doing all these necessary things anyway? Our attitude can be changed and it can start with a decision. Being aware of a problem is always the first step in solving it. Some people go through life never assessing themselves, never wanting to take the effort to improve themselves. But they miss the rewards and satisfaction of growth and improving their circumstances.

Sometimes we can increase our energy levels by regular exercise. We often don't need as much sleep if we can get regular, moderate exercise. Our bodies can become sluggish and tired if we have no exercise, making ourselves the target of lethargy. If on the other hand, we can get regular, moderate exercise our bodies become more efficient and our immune system is sharpened.

There may be times when one of you will want to stay home when the other wants to go out for dinner or something. It may not be for lethargy or apathy reasons. Men should always be encouraged in their romantic attempts, no matter how bad their timing is, or how impossible the circumstances are. Now and then, to accommodate both parties, there may be a need for adaptability and compromise. A person who is flexible can get along with nearly everyone. A person who is immovable in everything can get along with hardly anyone. So if one of you wishes to go out for dinner but the other doesn't for some reason, try a compromise. Have a romantic dinner at home with candles and music. Or let the person that wants to eat out, go and buy take away and bring it back to eat at home. Or plan to go out the next night when you can prepare for it. Accommodate the other person and you will enjoy the happiness of making them happy.

> *Men should always be encouraged in their romantic attempts, no matter how bad their timing is, or how impossible the circumstances are.*

One last point on apathy and lethargy. We are all allowed to be worn out once in a while for a good reason. But we can't have reasons every day. When it becomes constant we need to check our attitude and examine our priorities and workload. The opportunity we have today to spend with our lover or with our families will be gone tomorrow. And tomorrow comes very quickly. Sometimes there is no tomorrow and regrets are hard to live with. If a person feels lethargic but has the right attitude to make sure they will still enjoy an outing or an activity, and make the best of it, ninety-nine percent of the time they will be glad they went. Once you commit yourself to something, don't let others know they are going to pay for dragging you along. A happy person can be happy any place any time, he or she doesn't need certain prerequisites for places and times. Enjoy the time you have with your spouse, whatever the circumstances, and he will enjoy being with you, whatever the circumstances.

> *The opportunity we have today to spend with our lover or with our families will be gone tomorrow. And tomorrow comes very quickly.*

8. Setting Wrong Goals

Be careful that you don't set too high a goal for change in your man, or set too short a time frame for him to start doing romantic things. Make sure that your goals are realistic and attainable and don't expect him to be transformed instantly. The speed at which he climbs the steps may well be determined by your encouragement of each step he takes, as well as how much he enjoys the climbing. Accept him for what he is, love him as he is, and enjoy his small attempts. Make sure that you don't get frustrated with him by wanting him to be more romantic than his attempts have taken him. By pushing him or being frustrated you may well push him away from romance. Relax, give him time, encourage his attempts and keep your outlook positive. You may like to keep a record of the positive romantic things he has done to remind you of his progress and to keep a positive approach. Often it's only when we review the past that we understand how far we have come.

> *The speed at which he climbs the steps may well be determined by your encouragement of each step he takes, as well as how much he enjoys the climbing.*

It is easy to fall into the trap of nagging, or at least the man interprets it as nagging. But you can persistently remind without nagging. Nagging is negative. It is always an order, a threat, or a plea. But if you look for the positives, often the reverse side of the coin, and persist in those, you can accomplish your objectives. Take, for example, the woman who continually asks her man to mow the lawn. It is clothed in negative overtones, and she keeps reminding him he hasn't done it yet. The man sees the job as a chore and his lady as a nag. How does one turn it into a persistent positive? The woman could highlight how she appreciated it last time, how glad she is that her man cares for the lawns, even though he may not like the task. Or she might reveal how seeing him push a lawn mower turns her on (especially when he takes his shirt off) or she may even ask what she can do to help. By stroking a man's ego you get far more results than attacking him with negatives.

So it is with romance. Don't nag but persistently remind and encourage the positives. Remind him of the benefits and the satisfying feelings you have. Encourage his attempts and draw out the positives you wish to be repeated and don't forget to thank him for his past efforts. In this way you can be persistent, by keeping the idea of romance fresh in his mind without being perceived as nagging. Persistence, but it has to be positive persistence, is important, as the old saying agrees, "It's the squeaky wheel that gets the oil".

9. Opting For The Status Quo

The very fact that romance is a need for a woman and not a man, means that many men are often oblivious to its importance. And they will remain that way unless they have it explained to them. It is because women often find it difficult to express their romantic needs (so that a man can understand them) that men are never educated about the romantic needs of their partners.

It often happens that a man believes his relationship is fine, whilst his partner is frustrated by constantly reaching for his verbal responsiveness and trying desperately to connect with him at a deeper level. It is because a man will often opt for the status quo in the relationship, unwilling to change anything unless there is a definite need to change. A woman is sometimes amazed at how lax a man will be until she walks out the door. What is viewed by a woman as an end to a long drawn out death in a relationship is often viewed by a man as the beginning of doing something about it. By then it is usually too late. This contentment with past arrangements contrasts strongly with the female hunger to improve relationships and to constantly search for a deeper level of sharing and learning about one's partner.

> ***What is viewed by a woman as an end to a long drawn out death in a relationship is often viewed by a man as the beginning of doing something about it.***

Relationships often continue for ages with each partner acting out these conflicting views, and so the relationship never rises to the heights of its potential. Then, when women themselves cannot motivate their men, they too will often give up trying in a relationship and settle into the existing state of affairs, uncomfortable and unsatisfying as it may be for both of them. What is needed is for both parties to realise that although the easiest thing is to have the status quo in a relationship, a little effort can give a much preferred outcome. Maintaining the status quo can reduce the quality of the relationship to the lowest common denominator. This results in the following formulae.

MINIMAL EFFORT = STATUS QUO

OR

MINIMAL RELATIONSHIP

It is a simple formula, which can also be stated as, "you only get out what you put in". What women see is the minimal effort side of the formulae and complain that they feel their man doesn't love them because to them it looks as if he puts minimum effort into the relationship. Men on the other hand look at the minimal relationship or status quo and think, "No extra effort is required". He may complain at times that his needs in the relationship are not being met as well as he would like, but he doesn't see the other side of the equation as the real explanation.

What must take place is just a small change in the formula. When it is substituted to the following, a vast difference in outcomes take place.

A LITTLE EXTRA EFFORT (in the right area) =
ENHANCED RELATIONSHIP

OR

POTENTIAL RELATIONSHIP

Sometimes it is the capturing of the vision of an enhanced relationship that will motivate a man to put the extra effort in. The amazing thing about the above formulae is that by just making a small change, by adding a little effort, the end result is dramatically improved. The secret is educating a man as to what area is the right effort, as previous chapters have explored.

10. Inability To Commit

Once men have seen the improved end result they are more likely to be prepared to put the effort into it and make a commitment to it. Men must always have to know where the train is headed before they hop aboard. Let them see the superb destination and then they are prepared to not only pay the extra money for the ticket, but also to sit back and enjoy the ride. Once they see the value of their ticket they are more likely to pay the money. It is like buying a ticket to go down the street for $100 when you can go around the world for $150. The little bit of extra effort multiplies the result a hundred fold.

This is the big myth that men believe - "that increasing the quality of their intimate relationship is going to take more reserves of energy and money than they can muster". The truth is all it takes is a little bit of effort, and a little thought to work wonders in the relationship. What it does take is commitment. There is that one word that seems to drive so many men away, "commitment". The trouble for men is that it is such an open ended word. It is not defined enough for many men. To them it is like getting on a train that has a concealed destination. So they become so uncomfortable and so fearful of where they will end up that they forget that the relationship is the journey itself.

> *This is the big myth that men believe - "that increasing the quality of their intimate relationship is going to take more reserves of energy and money than they can muster".*

Spelling out what type of a commitment is needed, in a romantic relationship is the key to motivating men to hop aboard the train of romance. By making clear what the destination is by explaining how needs will be met on both sides, how enriched the relationship will be, and what exactly is required from him, the fear of commitment is removed and a man can relax and enjoy the benefits of an enriched relationship.

Once a man makes a commitment to put in extra effort in his relationship his whole attitude changes. He actually enjoys meeting his partner's needs and seeing the satisfaction he has created with just a little effort. All of a sudden he realises how easy it really is. Furthermore, he begins to live life at a deeper level, his outlook becomes more positive, his needs begin to get met and he can even deal with stress better. Eventually he realises that it has been his lack of commitment that has cost him this new enriched life for so long. This is the intimate relationship that everyone wants, but simply eludes so many.

There is a trend forming towards prenuptial agreements. Not only financial agreements but also clauses containing romantic, emotional and sexual commitments. These agreements can inspire greater awareness and commitment to meeting the other's needs but a prenuptial setting is not the only time these things can take place. Why not introduce new vows that both partners will commit themselves to each anniversary. These may reflect changing needs in a relationship, or a better awareness and deeper commitment to fulfilling your partner's needs. A very romantic exercise is for each partner to make up their own new vows and to read them out to the other each anniversary. Alternatively, you can both make them up together, after discussing each other's needs. Be sure to include romance in the vows as this can set the tone of the relationship for the months to come.

Some couples never get anywhere because they never talk about these things in a positive environment. When they do come up it is often under a negative atmosphere clouded with criticism, threats, demands and anger. They often either just accept the status quo, or believe the other person should just know instinctively what to do to fulfil every unvoiced need, but then get upset when those needs are not met. Talking about our needs in a relationship is so important and yet it is so rarely done in a positive way.

> *Talking about our needs in a relationship is so important and yet it is so rarely done in a positive way.*

Getting back to the journey analogy, some people can drive up and down the same street in their relationship all their lives, whilst all the time she would rather drive to Paris and he to London. Neither recognise the other's desires. The result is both get tired with a lot of effort and driving being done, but both are not getting to where they would like to go. Here are some guidelines tying it all together.

1. Set the destination clearly. Set aside time to exchange needs. Write down what you both would like to see more of in the relationship and then discuss and commit to how you are going to meet those needs.

2. Commit yourselves to enjoying the journey. A small commitment means a positive attitude. Charm is something that cannot be taught to a man. It comes naturally when he is relaxed, confident and has an incentive for the destination. A positive attitude and commitment to romance for example, will make giving a bunch of flowers an unforgettable experience. Why? Because of charm. Because the man wants to give it romantically and every part of his attempt says he loves you.

3. Stay on course. Steer the journey. In addition to sharing needs, you should also encourage efforts at meeting needs. Steering the relationship to the romantic, enriched destination requires not only an understanding of needs but also an affirmation when those needs are met. Both partners must affirm what they like in the relationship, affirm what they want more of in the relationship and continue to affirm rather than take it for granted. This affirmation provides the impetus to continue. It says that you are headed in the right direction and that it is the best place to go.

SUMMARY OF CHAPTER NINE

Be careful that criticism does not block romance. Give more appreciation.

Do not let anger rob you of romance.

Past conflicts must be resolved and not allowed to hurt the present.

Allow your partner freedom of will but avoid extremes in your relationship's power balance. Resolve conflict positively.

Stop sarcasm from yourself, others, and especially your man and do not play down your man's romantic attempts.

Depression will rob you of romance unless you deal with it.

Be aware of the negative effects of lethargy and apathy. Allow romance to motivate you.

Do not set the wrong goals or become frustrated at your man's lack of progress. Enjoy his attempts and continue to encourage him.

A man needs to understand that only a little bit of effort can make a dramatic improvement in his relationship.

The fear of commitment must be removed for a man, by clearly defining what is required of him.

Needs must be talked about in a ***positive*** way.

10

CHAPTER TEN

THE EXTRAS

"In order to be happy oneself it is necessary to make at least one other person happy." (Theodor Reik)

Friends

Our friends tell us a lot about ourselves without saying a word. When we begin to analyse it, we can understand why we have the type of friends we do. Sometimes friends are somehow lobbed on us as if they need us for some reason or another, and we are stuck with them, too gracious to refuse them. But the friends we choose, our closer, deeper friendships, are the ones that tell us about the type of people we are.

In life we are continually learning and absorbing information. Our friends become a source of information, personality and ethical exchange, whether we like it or not. When a person is young, they can be easily influenced by their friends. Sometimes it is even possible for them to be influenced to participate in uncharacteristic behaviour. But peer pressure is not only limited to adolescence. Later in life our immediate friends also influence us, even if it is in subtle ways.

What though, do your friends have to do with romance between you and your spouse? Well, if all your friends are positive towards romance they can only enhance and solidify your own romance. But if all of your friends are completely negative towards romance, you are going to find a dampener placed on your romantic flames. It may well be that your man will be influenced more by his unromantic friends, than you will be by yours. But the whole point is how compatible are your friends with your romantic approach to life? You need allies to support you and your romantic attitude, or at the least, not to work against you. You may not be able to instantly change all your friends, but you may minimise their negative impact by voicing your opinion to them, so that they know you are serious about romance, and that you won't tolerate them undermining you. You never know, when your friends see the results in your relationship, they could be converted to romance too. Try and increase friendships with people who are positive towards romance. Surround your spouse with people he enjoys being with, who are positively sold on romance as you are.

If you are genuinely looking for romantic allies then get a group of women together and go through the ideas in this book as a group. There are a variety of ways this can be done. You could read a chapter each week and then come together and discuss the ideas together. Or you could simply get together once a week and read a chapter together, stopping to talk about the ideas presented. You could even try out some of the ideas in your relationship and then report back to the group what you found most effective. This can provide support and encouragement and give different points of view to consider. It also keeps you on track and focused so you can push that romantic button on.

Couples

You not only have friendships as an individual, but you also have friendships as a couple. The friendships you have with other couples are important, because it can be a source of romance in itself. Think of the couples that you associate with, whom you feel completely at ease with, and really enjoy their company. It is true that whenever there are two adults together of the opposite sex there is an air of sexual chemistry that can vary in degree. You see not only your mate but other men too can appreciate you as a woman, and they can feel good just by being associated with you and being at ease. But you also can appreciate other men besides your spouse. This does not mean that you or your spouse are going to go and have an affair with these friends. What it means is that you acknowledge that there is a thing called sexual chemistry that operates between men and women. It is up to you as a couple to establish trust and to fix the boundaries in your relationship of what you both enjoy and are happy for the other to do. In a secure relationship where you have a relationship with other couples, whether it is doing things together, eating or going out together, or just simply visiting and talking about mutual interests, you can find it to be a source of stimulation, enjoyment and romance.

If you associate with romantic couples then you will easily be able to go out on romantic dinner dates with them. Some people really enjoy being with other people, while others prefer to be alone. But no matter what our preferences we can all enjoy another couple if we get on well with them.

You can introduce romance in your friendships with couples by a number of ways. Firstly, you can act as role models by being romantic yourselves. For example, you can touch each other in various ways that heighten romance while you are together. By caressing each other now and again while you talk you both can provide a role model of a romantic couple that acts as a lead for the other couple to follow. It also sends the signal that you are a happy, loving, secure couple and enjoy being together.

Secondly, you can also establish romance in your relationship by going out on romantic dinner dates. Getting into formal clothes and dining out is romantic in itself. By doing this you establish a romantic pattern so that it is natural for you all to share a romantic atmosphere at less formal times as well. Thirdly, the subjects of conversation can inject romance into the relationship you both have with other couples. If you are uninhibited in your conversations so that you all can feel free to express your views and relate stories on romantic topics, then you will enjoy the romance on this level.

After a romantic evening with another couple, it is common for a couple to be sexually more alive and ready for lovemaking when they return home. It is just that added sexual chemistry that can be controlled and used to your own advantage to heighten romance in your relationship with your spouse. In addition you will also be bringing romance into your friend's lives. As time goes by, you and your spouse may even be reminded of romance when the other couple lead out in being romantic. Some healthy, subtle competition of who is the most romantic may inspire both couples to keep their romantic fires burning brightly.

> *It is just that added sexual chemistry that can be controlled and used to your own advantage to heighten romance in your relationship with your spouse.*

Cultivate a Romantic Personality

Cultivating a romantic personality means making it easy for your man to romance you. It means that he would rather spend his time with you because your personality attracts him like a magnet. Something that stands out in people and what we long remember about them is a charismatic personality. What are the strengths and what are the weaknesses in your personality? Can you make a concerted effort to reduce your negative traits? One important aspect of a dazzling personality is that the person breathes optimism and knows how to smile. It is the successful, happy person that others want to be around. The person who only ever talks about their problems and complains about everything is always a burden to have around. People who are continually depressed can tire and tax your emotions. They push people away and sometimes are oblivious as to why they do not have many friends. People talk to us when we are prepared to talk to them about things **they** are interested in. Other people find it difficult to relate to us when all we can talk about is ourselves.

If you can cultivate an optimistic, cheerful personality that cares for others, then people will crave to be around you. Not only other people but also your man will enjoy his time with you as well. Thousands of men across our nation are frustrated at their women being depressed, irritable, moody and negative when their partners act in this way. What so many of these men do instead of working it through is withdraw. They withdraw into castles of silence designed to comfort them when their spouse is totally different to what they want them to be. This reaction though just increases the frustration a woman may experience at not being able to connect with her man.

Analyse the total trend of your disposition. Do your friends think you are a very positive woman? One thing you can do is never allow yourself a reason or excuse for being irritable or negative. People can change their whole outlook on life by a simple act of their will. Choose to be happy. Choose to be infectiously happy. Romantic people are happy because they have everything to live for. They have energy, purpose, commitment and most of all, love.

Never allow yourself a reason or excuse for being irritable or negative.

What a romantic, positive, caring person does, is loves people. Other people love them. Positive personalities make a clear distinction between people and things. They never treat people like things. We should love people and use things but unfortunately our lives are sometimes soured by a bad experience and we start to sour others by loving things and using people. Happiness we all know deep down inside is to do with our attitude and how we treat others. If suddenly you owned the whole world but there was not another human being to share it with, you would soon be lonely and bored. The essence of life is tied up in people, how we love those closest to us, what influence whether good or bad we have on others and whether we are prepared to invest in people rather than in things. If only we can realise this early rather than late in life we will be able to live a happy, wise life instead of one in search of elusive happiness.

The essence of life is tied up in people, how we love those closest to us, what influence whether good or bad we have on others and whether we are prepared to invest in people rather than in things.

Romance provides a good motivation to live life to the full, for taking the opportunities of each day and making each day special. Romance is positive, alive and warm. It can only change our lives for the better. Romance can give us hope in relationships and ourselves, it can mend hurts and break down walls. Make yourself an easy person to love and romance will flow into your life. Give up any attempts to change or manipulate your man through complaining. Be positive and loving setting the tone of the relationship by giving appreciation rather than demanding it. Provide a romantic lead in your relationship by cultivating a romantic, happy, loving, positive, feminine personality and watch the positive response it has on those closest to you, especially your man.

The Most Important Person To Love

It is very important to love your man with your whole heart but you deny your man your love if you can't love yourself first. To love yourself you must first of all accept yourself, just as you are. Remind yourself of how others love you and how you want the strongest power in the universe, love, to flow from you to others. Before this power of love can flow to others it must first conquer you. Accept the power of love, that love fills your entire being and is happy to reside in your every cell. Accept that you commit yourself to the ideals of love and that you are worthy of love - this incredible power of good in the universe. Once you accept that you are worthy of love then you can love yourself and then love your man and others. Picture yourself as a vessel full of love and you will have love to give throughout the day. Decide to let no one fill you with hate because that will only sour relationships you have with others. Love attracts love. Hate attracts hate. Both, if we allow them, can replace the other.

Self-Esteem

A woman who loves herself and reveals confidence attracts everyone, but especially men. A woman with confidence in herself can be romantic easily but a woman with low self-esteem will never reach the heights of romance she has the potential to attain until her self-esteem rises. When her self-esteem rises even just a little, then her capacity for romance will rise even more so. Romance does not leave room for non-acceptance. Romance from another is the ultimate of compliments because it is acceptance, it is the other wanting to share themselves with us. If our lover accepts us then we should accept ourselves. True love is unconditional and when we are accepted just as we are, it provides a base of stability for our loving in return. It means we can love unconditionally in return because we share the basic foundation in our relationship of acceptance. Being loved unconditionally does not mean we can do anything and get away with it. Rather it means we have a basis to change for the better because even if we fail we still have that foundation of unconditional love in our intimate relationship, motivating us to continue to love the other.

> *Romance from another is the ultimate of compliments because it is acceptance, it is the other wanting to share themselves with us.*

We can always improve ourselves and grow in a secure relationship where unconditional love is the basis. Unconditional love can provide that motivation to improve the areas in which we need to grow. Learn to accept and love yourself unconditionally. Learn to love your spouse unconditionally. Then watch the barriers to romance fall as love fills every corner of your life. Do your man a big favour - love yourself.

The Extra Mile

When I was studying for my degree, a large reading assignment was given to the class. I still remember one pragmatic student inquiring of the lecturer, "Will we be tested on this?" The response of the lecturer was, "Will it make any difference as to whether you study it or not?" He went on to comment with a smile, "What is it about students that they only want to learn what is examinable? Would it be so terrible for a student to learn something and then not be tested on it?" His comments provided an insight into human nature. So often in the school of life we aim at the minimum of what is expected of us. We do just enough to get by but we often forget the extras. Is it any wonder that life becomes routine and mundane? It is true that the best students read beyond the examinable reading that is set. They go beyond rote learning and understand the essence of the subject - not just the bare basics.

So often in the school of life we aim at the minimum of what is expected of us.

Going the extra distance in your relationship with your lover will make the difference between an average, contract based relationship and an uninhibited, loving, romantic one. Push yourself to deposit energy, love and thoughtfulness into your relationship and you will reap above average romance. Go beyond what your man expects of you and you will disarm him of his expectations. Go the extra distance and trust will replace any checklists.

Romance and Children

Couples sometimes find children are a real barrier to their romance. Children can on occasions, drain your time, energy, financial, emotional and physical resources but with some thought and planning you can preserve the life of your romance. When you start to think about it, the idea of children can be quite romantic at first. When a couple begin to plan to have a family they often get lost in the positives and ideals of parenting. The thought of creating a unique new life from the union of your love can be very romantic. The conceiving of a baby is certainly romantic and the excitement of feeling the baby move within you, while your partner places his hand on your abdomen, can also be very romantic. Even the birth of a new life can be romantic for both parents and the exploration of the little body to realise he has his father's eyes, fingers or toes. But there are other joys of childhood too, like teaching your child to walk, talk and become just like yourselves. Have I idealised children too much?

Sometimes a couple before they have children are blind to the realities and demands of parenting. But isn't it a little like love? Love is often blind in the early stages, before reality sets in. But the chores and demands shouldn't take away our happiness. Sure washing nappies, going without sleep at times, disciplining and arguing are not very romantic. But just as in marriage, it is good to dwell on the positives and remember some of the ideals we started with. Just recently, some friends tragically lost their little boy through a freak accident, and I'm sure they, as anyone, would be glad to have ten times the amount of soiled nappies and sleep deprivation, etc., if it would mean having their child back with them again. It all has to be kept in perspective, especially the unromantic times we have with our children. Keep an optimistic attitude to parenting and romance will not be destroyed.

Unfortunately, it is often only the mother that shares the joys of the positives of parenting. Some families' structure of parenting means that the father's major role in parenting is confined to disciplining. How often do you hear a mother threaten her child with, "Just wait until your father gets home"? Often a mother will call on her partner to babysit the children when she can no longer cope with them. This can be a time when the child might be continually upset and so the father only ever shares in negative interaction with his child. Men who fit this scenario need to share more in the positives of child raising, so that parenting becomes a joint concern and source of happiness and fulfilment. Often the mother is so burned out from the rigours of parenting that she has no reserves left for romance. It is important for children to see their parent's relationship as romantic, happy and positive, and for them to have fun times with both parents. You have a responsibility to pass on to the next generation a good role model of romance and love.

> *How often do you hear a mother threaten her child with, "Just wait until your father gets home"?*

So besides getting your mate to share in the positives of parenting, how can you increase romance? Here are a few suggestions. First of all, make sure that the two of you have time alone together. Then make sure that the time is quality time and that both of you enjoy it. This is time apart from when you go to bed. It is a time of togetherness that you need more than ever, if you suffer from the demands of parenting. Some couples make bedtime the only time they exclusively have together. You need time for growth and communicating apart from sex, otherwise you can soon lose the romance so that sex degenerates into the last chore of the day.

> *Some couples make bedtime the only time they exclusively have together.*

Unfortunately, some parents allow their offspring the privilege of sleeping all night in their parent's bed, which destroys even the last refuge a parent has left. Such habits are hard to break. An adequate lock on your bedroom door for when your children are older is a good security for romance and intimacy.

There are times when children can be included in romantic activities. Picnics and fun times should not be underestimated for their romantic effect. Time spent together in this way engenders closeness and strengthens family ties. Children can also copy the idea of romantic notes by writing their own love letters to their parents. The children can learn to be demonstrative in their love for their family members by joining in writing messages on the romantic message pad. You may like to even have two message pads. A private one for you and your lover, and another elsewhere, where the whole family can join in writing notes of appreciation and warmth to each other.

Romantic notes certainly come into their own when a couple are pressed for time by work and children. Including notes in lunch boxes or work areas for either partner can say, "I love you", when you are up to your eyes in stress. Taking the time to phone or text, even for a minute, during the day, can add romance to a demanding day and set the scene for romance to continue at home that night. Look for ways to be romantic, even as a parent and you will find many. Yes, parents can be romantics too.

Finally, if you are a parent, try and come to some agreement with friends who have children too. Instead of asking someone to babysit for you for nothing, or even for payment, try a swap in babysitting your children with your friend's. It is not too much of an extra burden to have an extra couple of children around for a few hours, especially if they get on well with your own children. In fact, sometimes the children can form good friendships and keep themselves amused even when it is your turn to babysit. Give yourself the luxury of having your children babysat for the whole night once in a while and indulge yourself in a second honeymoon for one night. Grandparents love the privilege and are thankful for the trust the parents show in allowing their grandchildren to stay with them. A break now and again can not only bring romance, but also give you a much needed break, leaving you fresh and relaxed for your children again.

Some communities even have babysitting clubs which work on a point system where you swap babysitting hours. Whatever way you work it, be sure to have time alone to inject romance into your parenting lives. It's not just an extra nicety, it's an absolute necessity!

A Romantic Calendar

Sometimes men can be unimaginative in their romantic attempts. Although wanting to be romantic, a man can still be hampered by a limited number of ideas and therefore he becomes repetitive and bored, or gives up. If this is your man's problem, you can give him a romantic calendar, which gives him a number of ideas to plan for. Below is a calendar I have included as a guide that you can copy and give to such a man. If you do not like some of the ideas you can omit them or add ones of your own. Make up your own whole calendar if you wish, but you may find yourself not trying different new, challenging things. I have included a space so that he can use it to date each idea when he carries it out, so that he does not repeat one idea to the exclusion of the others, without realising it. I have also included a column indicating a description of the cost, which can help in planning the activities. Remember it is the attitude you have in approaching such activities that will make them romantic. These are just some ideas, but you can make just about anything romantic if you are both committed to it.

Week	Suggestion	Date Carried Out	Cost
1	A candle lit dinner at home where the man cooks or is responsible for the meal.		Small
2	A window shopping stroll one evening.		None
3	At least five phone calls home where each partner tells how much he or she loves the other.		None
4	A picnic lunch in a park.		None
5	A movie at a cinema or drive-in.		Small
6	An evening talking of fantasies and discussing such statements as what you would buy if you won a million dollars that had to be exclusively spent on your partner.		None

7	The man does his partner's chores before bed and sends her to soak in a bubble bath.		None
8	The man has at last three baths or showers with his mate where he washes her and scrubs her back.		None
9	Dinner at a romantic restaurant.		Larger
10	A beautiful bouquet of flowers with a love note.		Small
11	A whole evening listening to music and just talking (best reserved for winter months).		None
12	A trip to the library to browse through books on love, sex and marriage (or a time searching these topics online)		None

13	A weekend or night away *without* the children.		Larger
14	A box of chocolates wrapped as a gift and given to the woman.		Small
15	A romantic card made by the man and posted, or given to the woman.		Small
16	An evening of looking through the wedding album or pictures at the early stages of your relationship and talking about the times you had when you were courting.		None
17	A few hours shopping together with the woman trying on lingerie or bathers and the man sharing his opinion.		Depends if any or how many are bought.

18	Making love romantically at a different venue.		None
19	Meeting for lunch at a cafe twice during the week.		Small
20	The man buys the woman some sexy underwear.		Small
21	The man volunteers to do the ironing or washing the clothes or dishes for one week (or some other chores he doesn't normally do).		None
22	The man organises a surprise date.		Variable
23	The man devotes three hours to attending to jobs needing attention around the home.		None
24	The man gets you "breakfast in bed".		None

25	The man sends a special love card.	Small
26	The man leaves at least five love notes for his partner to find during the week.	Small
27	Make two coupons and give them to each other to be used during the week.	None
28	Invite over to your place for dinner a young couple who are about to get married, and try to out-touch or out-kiss them.	Small
29	Tell your partner of your love for them through the medium of at least three different people this week.	None
30	A flower presented each day with a new verbal expression of your love for each other.	Small

31	Watch a romantic movie on Netflix or Amazon and enjoy an evening of popcorn and movies at home.		Small
32	The man pays for and organises a professional beauty treatment to pamper his lady.		Larger
33	A foot massage and manicure by each partner for the other.		None
34	Attend an event where *he* wants to go (eg. a sports event).		Variable
35	A bedroom party celebrating some significant date in your courtship or relationship.		None

36	Organise a photo session (or do it yourself) for you both, so you can update your purse and wallet photos of your spouse.	Variable
37	The man organises a mystery date just telling the woman the type of clothing needed and the time to be ready.	Variable
38	The man organises a river cruise.	Larger
39	Organise an outing where you pretend to meet for the first time.	Variable
40	Spend the morning at the zoo.	Small
41	Spend the day at an activity park and try as many rides as you can.	Larger
42	Spend the weekend away at the coast or lake.	Large

43	Visit a national park and enjoy the walks and views.	Small
44	Try an activity you haven't done before such as horse riding, water skiing, snorkelling, etc.	Variable
45	Ban the television set for the whole week and use the extra time for doing things together and playing games.	None
46	Spend some time relaxing in a hot spa together (at the gym, the public swimming pool or at some friend's place).	Small
47	Go parking one night in a romantic spot with a view of the city.	Small

48	Hold hands and undress each other with your other hand. Alternatively, make love with your clothes on and spend at least one hour in foreplay.	None (unless you rip your clothes!)
49	Order some pizza or fast food home delivered and eat it in bed (watch out for the crumbs!).	Variable
50	Play a game of strip jack or the loser of a game to perform a seductive strip to music (without either of you laughing!).	None
51	Enjoy an interactive games night playing things like charades, where there are no winners, just lots of fun.	None

52	One spouse to have a massage one night followed by the other spouse the same or next night.	None (unless you pay for a professional massage)

SUMMARY OF CHAPTER TEN

Encourage friendships that enhance romance.
Include activities with other romantic couples.
Cultivate a romantic personality. Be cheerful and optimistic so you attract rather than repel others.
Make yourself an easy person to love. Make it easy for your spouse to romance you.
Love yourself first, then let that love flow on to others.
The higher your self-esteem, the higher your capacity for romance.
Love your spouse and yourself unconditionally.
Go the extra distance in your relationship and reap the rewards.

Children can enhance romance by:
The excitement of childbirth.
Dwelling on the positives.
Appreciating the benefits of children before they grow up and leave home.
Including your man in the good times of parenting so that he isn't just a disciplinarian.
Remembering you have a responsibility to role model a happy, romantic relationship.
Making sure you still have time alone.
Including children in some romantic activities.

Including a special "family romantic pad" where feelings of affection and appreciation for family members are written. Remember the effect romantic notes have on your spouse. Swapping babysitting now and again.

Also,

Let your man have lots of ideas for romance including a romantic calendar.

CHAPTER ELEVEN

THE ROMANCE CONNECTION

"Your hand touching mine. This is how two galaxies collide." (Sanober Khan)

After all of the information we have looked at throughout this book let's return to the very first thoughts about the caveman found in chapter one. The first of the three aspects of the caveman was his confidence. The second was that his communication was limited. The third was his strength. All three of these characteristics are swirled around and overlap so that it's difficult to separate them when we address them. But what we will do now is discuss how these three traits all impact on romantic connection. We will look at the problems that happen naturally but also the solutions to turn around these traits that have ingrained themselves deep into human DNA so that a rich, lasting, romantic connection can be the core of your relationship.

CONFIDENCE

The first point made was that man was the hunter. His testosterone primed him to be ready in an instant for a fight or flight. He had a deep seated drive to tame nature, master the elements and know what he was doing. The corresponding trait that women today admire in a man is confidence. This affirms in a woman that she and her family will be well cared for and can help lower any anxiety she might have about the future.

The Problem

The problem is when the opposite of confidence is triggered. If a man loses his confidence he immediately begins to generate a whole range of negative emotions. The very worst thing that could possibly happen though is when his partner castrates his confidence. Unfortunately, many women do this continually without even realising it and the relationship becomes characterised by conflict and contempt. The key is understanding the opposite of confidence. The very opposite of confidence for men is known as ***shame***.

> *The very opposite of confidence for men is known as shame*

What adds fuel to the fire is that men are not really aware of how attuned they are, how sensitive they are of anything at all being interpreted as them not being good enough. This negative bias means they can hear a shaming statement in something that was never meant to be shaming. For example, when a woman says, "We need to talk about our relationship" a man hears "You are a bad partner". When a woman says, "There is a problem..." a man hears, "You're the problem." The opportunities are endless where a man interprets the message to mean he is inadequate, a failure, not good enough and doesn't possess the skills, ability and testosterone required to be a successful man. He simply feels shamed. He may not even be able to verbalise it in that way but all he knows is that he feels terrible.

What Happens

When the caveman was threatened, what happened? The first thing that occurred was that he felt an immediate surge of adrenaline and was ready for a fight! If that wasn't going to work then he would get out of there real quick! These two responses are activated instinctively still today whenever a man feels shamed, whenever he feels he has failed at something or whenever his manliness is called into question. Remember it doesn't have to be in fact, only in his own mind, his own perceptions. So whenever a man feels shamed he may immediately want to fight. He has all that adrenaline that has been activated so what is he going to do with it? Certainly not talk about it! In fact just the opposite. Although he may act angrily and want to win an argument almost at any cost and be seen to be right to restore his confidence again, he sometimes overreacts in trying to re-establish his confidence. The other important aspect of shame is that it makes you want to hide. That is the next thing the man is driven to do. He quickly looks for a man cave he can withdraw to so he can get out of the spotlight that has been shone on his overwhelming shame. Whenever a man feels inadequate in his relationship he feels shamed and the drive to fight or hide becomes extreme.

Enter Cortisol

Men have a hyper reflex towards an abrupt stimulus. It's in their DNA. If a tiger jumped out of the jungle suddenly without notice, the caveman would have to instantly be ready to harness his adrenaline and fight or run faster than the predator. If not, he wouldn't survive. However, that abrupt shock also initiates the release of another hormone in a man's body. It's called cortisol. It gets secreted during certain negative emotions. It's purpose is to get the man to do something to change things, to make them better. It makes a man very uncomfortable. It's that depressing, nagging feeling that just makes a man feel terrible. A man simply hates it. A man can instantly feel huge amounts surge through his body whenever he feels shame. This means he feels it whenever he is confronted with his woman's unhappiness or criticism. He instantly feels he is inadequate and so quickly enters adrenaline and dragging with it cortisol and shame.

When a man acts with emotional shutdown it is really an automatic defence mechanism designed to protect his masculinity, his adequacy, his confidence. It's to stop the shame from entering. If you don't feel anything, then you can't feel the shame of inadequacy. Sometimes he reacts with anger which is also another defence mechanism. If you numb the pain then it is also difficult to feel it. If you can blame others for it then you can divert the shame. Sometimes some men will revert back to primitive reactions of aggression where if he can take back control physically he won't feel the powerlessness of shame and failure. When a man argues with his partner strongly, he is trying to prove he is right to lower his toxic amount of shame. Whatever the reaction, as soon as a man feels shamed by his partner, no matter how good her intentions to get their relationship back on track, the man's defences become detrimental to the relationship and only serve to disconnect them from each other.

Some men are more sensitive than others to shame. It may be that the man grew up with a scolding mother that never praised him or never got excited about his achievements. It might be that his previous relationships with women followed a pattern that he felt he was never good enough for them. Or he may have felt constantly criticised over years. When these types of experiences occur, a man develops a very quick response of shame. If even a hint of shame is interpreted then this man will quickly come out fighting strongly or run away quickly to hide. In fact, many men have this default program of withdrawing from any conversation about their intimate relationship that might reflect poorly on them. When a man's neural pathways have been repeatedly stimulated over years, the deep grooves formed become instant reactions. Eventually, they see the worst in everything, even a compliment, and become severely depressed. Sometimes the neural pathway is so fast that the man has no idea what triggered his cortisol produced feelings of blah! He just is aware all of a sudden of feeling terrible. His partner might be nowhere in sight. But what has happened is that the repeated feelings of shame have now become expected, so much so that his brain is merely preempting the cause and producing the regular injection of cortisol. Such is the nature of repetition.

Harsh Start Up

John Gottman has studied intimate relationships for several decades. One of the things he came up with after these years of research was that if you used an abrupt start up in your interactions with your partner it's not going to end well. He was so confident that he made the hypothesis that he could predict with ninety percent accuracy which couples would be divorced a year or two later. The number one thing that women do to men to put the relationship on the path to divorce he called a "harsh start up". This simply means that a woman approaches the man with negativity immediately from the start. It might be a criticism that has been building up for a long time. It might be even a non-verbal cue such as withdrawing from intimacy or withdrawing from personal space. Even a banged plate in the sink whilst washing up could stimulate the fight or flight response and the bucket loads of cortisol, so imagine what a slammed door is going to do! A harsh start up also includes any attempt from you to complain about your relationship to your man.

> *A harsh start up also includes any attempt from you to complain about your relationship to your man.*

The Solution

Does this mean you can never talk to your man about what he does to annoy you in your relationship? Are men really that fragile? Well firstly it means that you need to avoid a harsh start up with your man. A man is not fragile, but his male ego, his masculinity and his confidence can be knocked very easily. And once that happens, self-protection cuts in, cortisol takes over and you lose the chance of a positive outcome in any conversation you wanted to have with him. John Gottman concluded that, "94% of the time, the way a discussion starts determines the way it will end." So to counteract the results of the harsh start up he promotes the soft start up. It means you won't jump straight in to judge or blame. It means you will use I statements rather than you statements and you will seek to close the distance between you rather than make it bigger. That's why at the dinner date back in chapter five you were asked to start with a series of questions. It wasn't launching into a series of attacks but rather it was positively focused. Questions such as, "What would you like more of in our relationship?", "What did you like about me when we first met?" and "When did you know you wanted to be with me for ever?" Even the question, "What do you think we could do to be happier together?" is an open ended question that places the control and the "valued opinion" back on your partner rather than shaming him from telling him he is not good enough because he has not been living up to your expectations. The harsh start up verses the soft start up is only a small change in approach but it results in totally different conclusions. The conversation ends up discussing the same information and topics, it's just that it doesn't get hijacked by cortisol. It also means that instead of making distance between the two of you, you can end up closing the distance and become connected, not disconnected over the discussion of the same topic of conversation.

STRUGGLING WITH COMMUNICATION

In the first chapter we likened the caveman's communication skills to grunts. Whilst some men are very good communicators, many traditionally struggle with deeper exploration of feelings, talking about relationships and intimacy tolerance. Part of the reason is that talking about these things are bound to stimulate their fear of being inadequate and will therefore in their minds make them end up feeling shamed. It's "best to give that cortisol overdose a very wide birth" he reasons, "so let's not go anywhere near those areas". Men can increase their intimacy tolerance but shame has to be guaranteed to not be allowed out of the box.

The Problem

Although the saying goes "No man is an island", many men instinctively try to prove this quote wrong when it comes to sharing at an emotional level. If a man were to appear in any way needy, doesn't that mean that he is not sufficient by himself to be a real man? So any hint of going deeper emotionally can quickly have the brakes slammed on by his fear of self-inflicted shame and feelings of inadequacy. Vulnerability is unfortunately the direct opposite trait you would want if you are trying to be a caveman. Think of an elephant being afraid of a mouse. It doesn't realise it doesn't have to be afraid, but it still is afraid. Think of your big strong man being afraid of connecting with his emotions without his weapons of adrenaline and strength, and without his getaway car engine running for him to make his escape quickly and allude the danger. Men have none of these allies to rely on if they commit to talking about their vulnerabilities, emotions and their intimate relationship. The fight or flight response makes things worse for them. So what else can they rely on? They've exhausted their bag of tricks! They've got nothing. Nothing that is familiar that is.

> *Vulnerability is unfortunately the direct opposite trait you would want if you are trying to be a caveman.*

The Solution

Back in chapter one we mentioned how women bond through speech. When women get together they derive satisfaction from talking to their girlfriends about themselves, relationships and other people. But what do men do with other men? What do they enjoy and naturally talk about when together with other men? This is a major difference between men and women. Ever noticed how most men tend to congregate together at parties or functions and most women tend to form their own groups as well? Most men aren't really interested in other men's deepest fears or how they are getting on with their intimate partner. In fact if a man were to start talking about his fights with his woman to his mates many would not know how to react, would feel uncomfortable and want to change the subject very quickly. Culture is changing and men are learning how to check on their mates to make sure their mental health is okay. But you get the point. What men are more likely to do with their mates when they are young at least is play sports or games. Later they will often watch sport together. When they talk it is often about sport or their other wins or their achievements. The caveman is still alive and well. Men love to talk about winning and achieving, whether it is about work or play. The lesson here is that you can't plunge straight into a conversation with a man about your relationship. You can't rip the DNA out of his body. You can't change him. You have to work with what you've got.

While a woman connects through talk with other women, she has to adapt to how a man connects. When a man plays a sport he is in the active mode of doing, not speaking. He uses his caveman DNA to focus his concentration, skills and abilities. If playing a team sport he bonds with his team mates by scoring a goal, winning, or hitting a home run.

He feels great if he wins the admiration of his team mates when he clearly contributes to the winning performance of the team. If he is playing an individual sport such as golf, he is still competing against the elements as he battles against the course. This act of "doing" is a physical act. Physical things are where the man is attuned to. He is at home in the world of physicality. So the solution is for a woman to start with touch. A man is usually pleasured by touch. Think of back in chapter four how we talked about a man's primary fantasy. It was access to as many beautiful women as possible to adore and desire him. Think about the images pandering to this male fantasy in Hollywood movies. In historical ones it used to be images of kings being caressed, fanned and fed by scantily clad women whilst reclining on a couch. These days it is more likely to be a gangster in a hot tub surrounded by naked women who still caress the man at the centre of their attention and supposed affection. These images are still consistent with a man's strong drive to be touched by the woman he loves and also be desired by her. If he has that, then his masculinity is "proved" beyond all doubt. Sex is the deepest physical connection a man can experience. It is because of this a woman needs to enter through the door way of physical touch to get to her man. Trying to bash through a brick wall with conversation to get through to a man about his relationship doesn't work, his defensive walls are always reinforced.

So the solution is for a woman to start with touch.

I am not saying a man has to have sex to get to a deeper level of communication. What I am saying is that a woman needs to know how to touch her man affectionately more in order to connect. Talking to a man does not connect. Talking to her girlfriends will connect a woman to other women, but won't work when talking to her man. Think about it. When you regularly, affectionately touch your man in the course of your interactions, outside of sex, you send the following messages, "I like you, I like having you here, I like touching you, I feel safe with you, you and I are connected." When a man receives this message he can relax. He doesn't have to be constantly vigilant waiting to be hyper aroused from the next abrupt start up shaming him that he has got to do better in his relationship. Why? Because he feels connected already, and when you feel connected you can relax and go deeper without feeling the need to defend yourself.

The majority of long term relationships tend to suffer from a cutaneous deprivation (I love that term. It just means a lack of skin to skin touch). Now there are several reasons why touch decreases over the long term in intimate relationships. We have looked at many of them in this book. One of them is that it has been set up in many relationships as one dimensional. That is, it has been associated with sex so many times previously that whenever a man touches his partner, the non-verbal message is that he wants sex. Because of this, a woman often over the years sets up an almost instant aversion to it when mercy sex and intercourse estrangement has dominated the relationship (see chapter seven). So she reasons she's no way going to start touching her partner or he will be all over her like a rash! So she pulls away, even though when they first met, they were both all over each other like a rash. Another reason is that conflict increases the distance and decreases the touching between a couple. So if the woman, for instance, is frustrated at the level of emotional connection she is getting from her man, the connection itself and hence the touching, decreases.

The Chemical Connection

Think of the feelings a mother has towards her baby when she is relaxed and breastfeeding her baby. In order for her to breastfeed she has to be relaxed. She then has to connect the baby to herself. The baby's outer mouth has to physically touch the breast and then as it muzzles in, the baby's reflex takes over and he or she attaches his or her mouth to the nipple. But there is also another reflex taking place in the mother. As the baby suckles from her breast, oxytocin rushes into the mother's bloodstream which releases the milk. The hormone creates feelings of bonding, nurturing, connecting and generally good feelings in the mother. There has been lots said over the years about mothers touching and cuddling their babies. Babies have even been starved of maternal touch in experiments back in the 1960s to find out how screwed up it would make the kids! Of course they also did the same experiments with monkeys and decided the ones that died did so because of cutaneous deprivation (there's that great term again). The whole point is that we need human touch. It's actually a lot more important than we realised previously and those who suffer from being deprived of it crave it so deeply they sometimes do crazy things.

I have been trained in a few different professions in my life. They all tend to circle around the people-helping professions. I have worked as a paramedic for over twenty-five years and it has taught me some amazing lessons about touch. Some people I came across in my work as a paramedic were so deprived of human touch they would go to excessive lengths to try and fabricate it. Some patients would feign medical conditions including unconsciousness. They would accidentally on purpose collapse crossing a busy road in the middle of a bustling city at peak hour. It's like the whole city would go into shut down as people flocked around the patient faking it. People from everywhere would rush to their aid, cushion their head, hold their hands and give words of comfort. One woman called an ambulance one night in the city I worked and when we arrived the best she could come up with was that she needed help to organise her fruit in her fridge. I talked with her for half an hour, talked to her about her loneliness and her estrangement from her son and then eventually left after both my partner and I gave her a long hug. Looking back I think we probably helped her far more than we realised. She never called back as far as I was aware and I never saw her again. Another patient I saw in the emergency department was a regular patient who sometimes called for an ambulance multiple times a week. There were new staff on however who were unaware of her history. She put on such a convincing act that she was even intubated (this is where a tube is placed down your throat and into your windpipe to secure your airway so that no matter what happens at least you will keep getting air, even if the breathing has to be done for you). Normally a patient would be sedated, however she was so good at acting sedation wasn't needed. They just pulled her head back and shoved the tube straight down there and she didn't even wince. The masquerade continued until a more senior doctor became involved. He soon pulled the tube out and got her straight up and kicked her out of the hospital all within a couple of minutes. These are all examples of people with pathological conditions who will go to great lengths to force people to care for them and touch them. For some of the regular patients at emergency departments it's the only time they get other people to touch them. They are usually estranged from their relatives and friends, often socially obnoxious without even being aware of it but still crave human touch.

Seeing I am giving examples of touch from my work as a paramedic I want to share with you a very personal experience I had with a patient who taught me an amazing lesson about touch that I will never forget. Whilst the other examples were pathological in nature (meaning they were basically sick puppies who needed psychological help) this one came from a woman who truly knew the power of touch. It was about 2 pm in the afternoon and I had been so far busy all day. My partner and I were yet to try and get something to eat so we weren't in a completely happy and optimistic mood. At the end of our case we immediately got our next call. It turned out to be a woman in her thirties who was being sent home to die. She had been given hours, not days to live. I felt like this was to be a burden to me. Why was a paramedic crew needed for a job like this? There were transport crews who could have taken this call. It's also one of those jobs that is really difficult and can sap a lot of mental energy out of you. I mean what can you say to such a patient? "Hi we're here to take you home to die, isn't it a lovely day?" So we marched in with some formal but sombre greetings and then transferred her to the ambulance stretcher. I didn't say much and I had my head down fastening her seat belts. She could sense that I wasn't in the mood for connection. I am sure she realised I was uncomfortable with her plight and my intention was to make sure I kept my distance from her emotionally. But that suddenly all got thrown out of the window.

She simply grabbed my forearm and forced my eye contact. She then just looked me in the eye and said she wanted to thank me so much for what I was doing. Everything instantly changed for me. There I was intentionally trying to keep my distance but within a moment of touch she connected with me so deeply, so beautifully, so meaningfully that she had my complete and absolute attention. The touch was something I can't describe or even begin to verbalise but it was a touch that went deep into my soul. Although in an emaciated body ravaged by the final stages of terminal cancer, weighing only around 40 kilos (88 pounds), I connected with a young woman with a wonderful, vibrant and caring personality. We didn't stop talking for the half hour trip on her last journey home. I laughed with her, I cried with her, I understood her and she understood me. I finally wheeled her inside to her bedroom, met her husband and then sat on her bed still in deep conversation with her. I didn't want to leave. I talked some more. I felt guilty I was taking up her precious time with her husband but she wanted me to stay. Her husband could see she was enjoying the time. She asked her husband to get me a promotional baseball cap she had been given from her now retired workplace. I accepted it gracefully and finally dragged myself away to reluctantly go and eat some lunch.

I couldn't stop thinking about this remarkable encounter with this stranger. She had been a stranger to me only a couple of hours earlier but now I felt an amazing connection with her like I had known her for years. I couldn't help myself but I was compelled to go back to her house the next day when I was off duty. I knocked on the door and met her young teenage daughter. She got her father who then informed me his wife had passed away two hours after I had left her. This beautiful human being in her last hours on earth took the initiative to connect with a stranger. Someone who was distant. She could not have been without pain. She could not have been without her fears. But in that time she taught me the power of connection through touch. I never forgot her. I never forgot the lesson she taught me about touch. In my time since our meeting I have tried at times to model what she taught me. Even though we were two strangers she was able to connect us deeply in an instant. In the years since then I have seen people in all sorts of crises and desperate situations suddenly connect through a compassionate touch. Whether it is a hug, holding a hand or an arm around a shoulder, I have seen the power of human touch again and again. This woman and I quickly bonded and our communication was boosted straight to level five where there is complete knowing and communing with each other. Touch is powerful and unfortunately we constantly hear of inappropriate and abusive touching which devastates lives. It is a powerful thing, but it can be used positively and powerfully between people and especially people who love each other.

Although the above examples illustrate touch between strangers and its power to connect and fulfil the need we all have, the principle is exactly the same when it comes to intimate touch. Used in the correct way, compassionate touch can bridge the connection gap. If programming has raised barriers to touch making the person cynical as to its intention it can be refused and blocked. But when a lover is genuinely trying to establish connection through gentle, pleasurable touch, the result can be amazing. Touch which has no resistance, is welcomed, is allowed to pleasure the recipient and is then reciprocated can be a thoroughly connecting experience. So the bottom line when trying to get your partner to go deeper emotionally is touch first, speak last. Think connection not conversation.

> ***Think connection not conversation.***

This is proven to be true when we think of when people first fall in love. Their lives are filled with romance, love and especially connection. They don't have to have mediators to communicate messages to each other. They aren't constantly confused about mixed messages. They get each other. They don't need to attend communication workshops in order to communicate with each other. The reason is all because they are connected, so they have little trouble communicating with each other. If they are not connected with each other then all the communication skills are of little value, they just tend to argue better. Patrica Love and Steven Stosny tell the story of how they would spend lots of time with couples trying to improve their communication in an attempt to get them to reconnect. There was a big emphasis on communication skills in couples' therapy especially in the eighties and nineties. However, they weren't seeing the success they hoped for. But they began to realise they were getting things around the wrong way. They came to understand couples in trouble were not disconnected because they have poor communication; they have poor communication because they are disconnected. They wrote what I consider to be one of the best books on relationship improvement called, "Why Women Talk and Men Walk, How to Improve Your Relationship without Discussing it." I will quote more from it in the next section but for now think about a major point they make in their book. Think connection, not communication. This is especially good information for a woman. If you lead with communication you are most likely going to encounter a man's defensive barricades or he will shut down. Concentrate on connection and the communication will be so much easier. I have added a powerful way to build connection with a man which is through caressing touch. Build this into your relationship first so that it comes naturally and often and you will find it a great bridge to building intimacy.

One more point needs to be made about building and increasing intimacy through touch. Once your relationship is completely at ease with touch for touching's sake, **then** you can start to blend conversation with it to build intimacy and increase your partner's intimacy tolerance. Talk about the good things your man does. Talk about the good things you enjoy in your relationship and how you want more of those things. Don't become critical or demanding. Go with the flow and keep that connection. Couples who master this connection and intimacy connection and who increase their intimacy tolerance are able to do something quite special. They can actually talk during lovemaking and even the man can feel right at home talking throughout their ultimate physical bonding. They can look into each other's eyes and soul during lovemaking and completely connect without fear or any self-consciousness. They don't block out the emotional connection during lovemaking by keeping their eyes tightly shut. Instead they open up completely to their partner and invite their partner deep into their heart. That is unreserved connection.

Many relationships get it so wrong. They tend to have no touching at all unless it's during sex. Then when they are having sex neither of them says anything. It's like they are actually disconnected for the rest of their relationship outside the bedroom but allow themselves to connect to a shallow degree for the sake of sex. The deep kissing often only happens in the bedroom and then often doesn't even happen at all in many long term relationships. Now think of what we have just been exploring. Think about your relationship as being one that experiences connection at a deep level most of the time. Think about you both initiating touch in the form of a gentle caress as you pass each other which just lets the other know you notice each other and you are connected. Think about you both being able to deep kiss passionately outside the bedroom just because you can and it doesn't have to lead to sex (every time)! Think about how you both could talk about your love to each other during lovemaking and look into each other's eyes during climax. Think about how both of you could talk to the other about anything and be assured that your partner has your back, will protect you and would do nothing to hurt you. Now that is romance! That is romantic connection. Let's look now at that third characteristic of the caveman and especially look at what it means and what impact it has on a woman.

STRENGTH – HAS MUSCLES

The caveman was the protector. His higher testosterone levels meant he could build muscle mass and was strong in comparison to the cave woman. He wasn't sitting on a chair at an office desk all day. He had the elements to tame and hunting to keep him occupied. He was actively doing things.

The Problem

Having a strong man doesn't equate to a man being an impregnable fortress in a woman's mind. The image in a woman's mind about having a strong man is one of **protector**. What appeals to a woman about a strong man is that she can feel safe with him. If she feels safe with him, this means she can trust him and relax her fears. That trust and feeling safe for a woman is something that the majority of men don't get. Men don't naturally feel scared walking down a city street at night by themselves like a woman would. A man might even welcome an opportunity to physically fight with another man if the odds were in his favour and he had someone watching that he might want to impress. To back down from a fight might even cause a man greater pain than losing the fight because his shame would be activated if he were to retreat like a coward from a fight. Now this a woman doesn't understand, but it's true.

But while the caveman might have been able to protect his woman with his strength, today's man has to protect his woman with skills other than physical prowess and bulging muscles. Today's man is challenged not only with making his woman feel safe and secure in their environment, but he is challenged with making her feel safe and secure **in their relationship**. Testosterone, adrenaline and the stress responses in the man end up becoming the initiation of feelings of insecurity, anxiety and distrust in the woman. Think about it. When a man starts to feel shame in his relationship he can either fight or withdraw. Fighting only increases the conflict between a couple which increases the insecurity in his woman. If he withdraws instead, this still frustrates the woman because now she feels abandoned which also increases her insecurity. So his strength doesn't help him close the gap when things go belly up, all his known tricks actually make things worse.

As Pat Love and Steven Stosny point out, couples get caught in cycles of activating their partner's sore points. When a woman isn't getting out of her relationship what she needs, she feels distant and it triggers her anxiety. When a woman feels close she can relax; when she feels distant, she gets anxious.[27] The problem is when a woman is upset about her relationship what does she do to try and fix it? She does what is natural to her. She does what she would do with her girlfriends, she tries to talk about it. However, when she tries to talk about her relationship with her man, he wants to either win the argument and prove he is right, that he is not to blame, that he is adequate as a man in the relationship, or he shuts her down by stonewalling or withdrawing. The whole cycle is that a woman feeling insecure in her relationship stimulates a man's dread of feeling shame and a man feeling shame in his relationship stimulates a woman's insecurities in their relationship. Both try to fix the problem, but the way they both go about it throws fuel on each other's fire of torment.

The Solution

When men feel stressed it means they are in a state of hyper arousal. This means cortisol is being pumped into their bloodstream. They are ready for a fight or ready to run, neither of which are suited to enhancing bonding. This means that stress at work or road rage experienced on the way home have already engineered the man arriving home to have the same results a harsh start up would cause him. When a woman feels insecure she wants to feel closer to her partner so her fears are eradicated. However, if she asks for a conversation on making their relationship better, she loses her man to cortisol induced fight or flight. The secret is to re-frame what she is desiring into caveman language. What the caveman is familiar with is his strength and what he can do with his strength. What the caveman can do is **protect**. Rather than ask for a conversation about their relationship the woman needs to ask for her big strong man's protection. This is where she becomes vulnerable and needs protection. This is something the caveman knows to do instinctively and easily. Plus because there is no threat to him he can protect without adrenaline and cortisol taking over. By seeking protection the woman does a number of things. She stops the release of toxic cortisol. But she also closes the distance between the two both physically and emotionally. The response is something a man can do. It has a physical component. He naturally takes a closer stance to his woman to protect her. He puts his arm around her. He naturally closes the distance because he is not being attacked by her. He reassures her that everything will be okay. But something else happens in the process. When the two come together in a physical bond, oxytocin begins to get released. So not only does the cortisol go down but the oxytocin goes up. This chemical reaction is the exact opposite of what often happens when a couple trigger each other's sore points and it escalates into full blown warfare. On the contrary, by closing the distance and asking for protection it makes whatever the issue a shared, joint problem, not an issue that just one side has.

> *Rather than ask for a conversation about their relationship the woman needs to ask for her big strong man's protection.*

The bridge where both the man and the woman need to meet is compassion. Protection in the man triggers compassion in a man. Once a man is compassionate to his woman, cortisol drops, oxytocin rises and he feels connected to her. He can still feel confident as a protector and so his shame will not be triggered. When a man protects, his woman naturally feels safer, her cortisol drops, she feels more connected and her oxytocin starts to rise. As her oxytocin rises, her natural cave woman traits of nurture and compassion come to the fore and she feels connected. The bottom line is that a couple can get through virtually anything if they both feel connected and bonded to each other. If each other's shame and insecurity are activated by harsh start ups, criticism, defensiveness, blame, withdrawal, cortisol and adrenaline surges, disconnection will be assured every time, ultimately resulting in divorce.

So let's look at the formula for a woman wanting her fears and insecurities in her relationship addressed. Lower the cortisol. Be aware of the last 30 minutes your man has experienced. Is he frustrated, annoyed, angry already? Reset. Do something together or let him do something alone if necessary. Get rid of the adrenaline, do a workout, do something physical. Then seek to touch lovingly. Seek to connect, don't talk. Thirdly, and only after several minutes, tell your strong man you are feeling insecure and you need him to protect you. This will allow him to connect with you and feel like he can do something for you. He can move to protect you from feeling insecure. This means his compassion for you is activated. He will seek to connect rather than rush into fight or flight mode. Rather than say, "I need you to protect me more," say, "I am feeling insecure and need your protection." Or instead of saying "you make me afraid", say "I feel afraid, I need reassurance". This becomes a shared place of connection so the two of you are together facing whatever the problem happens to be. When you approach, hold firm in your mind the picture of your spouse caring and compassionate towards you. Hold firm the picture of him from when you felt most connected to him. He is still this same person. Talk to that person, hold that person, connect to that person.

A modern man no longer has to protect his woman from wolves, but he does have to learn to protect his woman from feeling insecure. A man that takes the lead in romance does exactly that. A romantic man makes his partner feel special, makes her realise he thinks of her when they are apart and makes her able to trust him. This is the power of romantic connection. This also explains why honesty is so important to a woman in her relationship. If she can completely trust a man then she is secure in her relationship. There are no unanswered questions continually plaguing her. She is freed up from any anxiety to completely bond with her man. But wait there's more.

A modern man no longer has to protect his woman from wolves, but he does have to learn to protect his woman from feeling insecure.

Telomeres and Romance

In 2009 Elizabeth Blackburn won the Nobel Prize in biology for her discovery and research of telomeres. Telomeres are the caps on the ends of DNA. They are likened to caps on the ends of shoelaces which keep the shoelaces from becoming frayed over time. It's important that these caps stay intact because they protect the rest of the DNA. The greater the telomeres break down then the greater the risk of DNA death, which results in the death of the cell. As cells divide and age the telomeres become shorter. The shorter your telomeres the higher your chance of heart disease, cancer, susceptibility to infection and death. Something that is very interesting is that Blackburn discovered that stress, especially chronic stress made the telomeres shorter. It seems the hyper arousal of cortisol and adrenaline repeated over time attacks the telomeres viciously. Furthermore, there were two types of stress in particular. One was how we perceive stress and tend to ramp it up so it gets a greater response from us than the threat deserves. I think of this as a male stress response in fight or flight that gives a greater response than what is proportionately needed (like when someone cuts you off on the freeway and you go into road rage). The second type is called ruminating stress where your mind goes over and over the thing causing you stress as you relive it a thousand times when you are lying in bed wide awake instead of sleeping soundly. This one I associate more with a woman's response to when she is unhappy in her relationship. Both types can be experienced by either gender and both types produce cortisol and affect the ends of your DNA strands called telomeres. Both types lead to disease and death. Both types impact negatively on your romantic relationship and emotional connection.

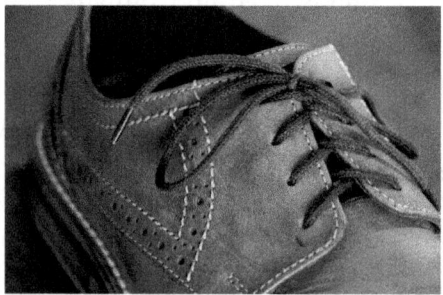

The good news is that telomeres can be repaired. It has been found that cancer cells generate telomerase which is an enzyme which keeps repairing the ends of the DNA. In this way the cancer cells continue to divide and grow, not ageing or dying which is not good news for the patient. So there's all this research now looking at telomerase and how it could be the next anti-ageing drug compound. Okay so where are we going with all this? Blackburn herself concludes that compassionate caring for others can actually rejuvenate the telomeres. Her co-author, Dr Elissa Epel also adds that connecting with others and helping others can prolong lives.[28] Another study has found that women who practised loving kindness meditation, a technique that encourages compassion, had longer telomeres than women who didn't.[29] You can go and get your telomere length tested easily enough to see what your biological age is. There are several companies that offer it cheaply enough. But more importantly, more compassion will lengthen them whatever length they are at the moment. Unhealthy stress responses are literally and biologically killing us. Compassion on the other hand, practised regularly in our most important relationship will add years to our life and life to our years. When we live bonded together and practising compassion in our relationship, we actually reap health benefits as well as fulfilling deep emotional needs. Compassion must replace cortisol if we want a romantic, connected relationship. It just turns out that the side benefit is that it's also far better for our physical health as well.

> *Compassion must replace cortisol if we want a romantic, connected relationship.*

Negative Mind Wandering and Selfing

When we have negative experiences during our day they don't remain in the past. We tend to carry them with us by hanging on to them. We think about them often by ruminating over them deceiving ourselves that we are somehow problem solving them. Think about a couple who come home who have both experienced some stressful situations in their day. Then they make a conscious effort to connect. They sit down, they might touch each other, hug, hold hands or something similar in order to genuinely connect. As they talk and listen to each other both experience a mind wander of a certain rating. In their mind they are somewhere on a scale which indicates how much they want to be present in that moment. Think about where this couple might both be on the scale. He might be at say 40 out of 100, she might be at say 60. The fact that neither can be completely present in that moment indicates their barrier to be completely connected. By both of them rejecting the present attempts to connect by a certain amount means they are adding stress to their connecting, even though they are both making the effort to intentionally connect. By rejecting their present experience even in part, instead of fully embracing the present they are in fact creating additional stress for their environment without even being aware of it. Whenever we begin to reject our present experience by thinking about stressful, past experiences or future anxieties we sabotage our present, including our present attempts to connect no matter how good they are.

Not staying in the present is a form of suffering. Many of us don't see it that way but we need to. It is a real source of unhappiness. We have a bad experience during the day and then we keep drifting back to it whenever we become still. Usually this is when we stop, when we close our eyes to sleep (or when our partner is dominating the conversation). The fact is though, the more we can live in the present, the more we can accept reality, the happier we become. Part of the mind wandering to past negative experiences Dr Elissa Epel calls "selfing". This is because all of our negative thoughts are around our self. We try and change the past in our minds, or we go over and over the same ground which we think is helping us. Instead it is killing us and our relationships. Let it go. How do you do that? Mindfulness is one way. Mental training to turn your thoughts to more positive areas is another. But hang on a minute, what about compassion? What's fascinating is that the practice of compassion actually short circuits "selfing" because it gets our focus off ourselves and puts it on the other person. This is yet another reason why the practice of compassion is so important when we attempt to connect with our spouse. When you hold positive thoughts in your mind about your partner, you lower the stress from intrusive, stressful "selfing" thoughts that would otherwise steal your focus and positivity. Being compassionate towards your partner allows you the opportunity to halt your negative mind wandering and become truly connected in the moment with the person you love. But without the stance of compassion, it will become hijacked to stress responses so easily which are counterproductive to emotional bonding and connecting. It just happens that when we can let go and experience compassionate caring for others our telomeres grow longer as a great side effect. Single people can also gain these benefits by compassionate connecting with others. It's just that a couple has that opportunity every day. Whether it is a man or a woman, compassion makes us more protective rather than controlling.

Not staying in the present is a form of suffering.

Giving Compassion At The Most Difficult Time

So you get the importance of connection. You get the idea of compassion. You understand how stress responses work to stop both of them. But how do you connect and show compassion when you're angry with your partner? Isn't that the real challenge? Firstly, the more we practise connecting and compassion, the easier it becomes. The more we get used to doing it, the more natural it becomes even in times of stress and conflict. Three strategies are important to exercise compassion in the more difficult times.

Strategy One - Commitment

The first one is commitment. Commitment used to keep people together for years even when they disliked each other. Now because divorce is so much easier than say sixty years ago, people don't tend to hang around when they can get a divorce and move on. However, people don't get divorced after every argument. After tempers cool down and strong negative feelings subside, couples often find their way back to each other. There are times though when all of us get angry and might in the moment *feel* like leaving the relationship. But that feeling is usually transitory. It changes and then we makeup and have different feelings towards our partner. Commitment realises and accepts that negative feelings towards our partner will come and go much like a lot of stresses in our life. But commitment grounds us in the **decision** that we are in this for the long haul. That decision gives us a foundation that feelings do change, but a decision can be more solid regardless of the changing environment.

The trick is to commit to connecting and reconnecting. Make it intentional. Keep it in focus. This is so even when you don't feel like connecting, you still can. One exercise I encourage you to do with your partner is to practise what I call "fight time". It can be a lot of fun but it is designed to help you find a way back when you get disconnected. It goes like this. You both commit to a **staged** verbal fight. Pick an unreal subject, not one too close to home, certainly not one you fight about often. You can build up to that in time. Baby steps for now. Once you pick the topic you have turns at who will initiate re-connection first. The key is in the acting. You can be animated, you can shout, you can even name call but you can't hurt the other or destroy the other person verbally. Keep it reasonably low key and decide on a time limit for the fighting period. Two minutes would be more than enough. After the two minutes the designated "re-connector" has to initiate re-connection. Some resistance is allowed against the connection attempts by the other partner to make it more realistic but watch out because pay back is a bitch! Once the re-connection is complete and accepted the exercise is over and then the roles are reversed. The resister becomes the one initiating connection. At the end of the two part exercise the couple can talk about their experiences and how they felt acting in the scenario. They can even score each other out of ten and try to get a higher score next time. You might even want to go all the way with this exercise and act out makeup sex which some couples find very passionate! It's also a good thing too for each to explain how compassion featured in their re-connection and what visualisation of their partner each had in their minds when they were attempting the re-connection.

This fascinating exercise is something unique. Conflicts will always come. They are inevitable. So why not practise finding our way back to our lover so we get really, really good at it? Done in the right spirit, by a couple that can connect, this exercise can actually be a lot of fun. But it also gives the couple some tools at coming back from conflict when trying to get back together when they are both terribly wounded from a huge battle. Laying down neural pathways by repeating them, make them more automatic and easier to accomplish. Besides, who wants to stay mad at each other for days when you could be back together really quickly because you are proficient at finding your way back to your connected state so quickly?

> *So why not practise finding our way back to our lover so we get really, really good at it?*

Strategy Two – Create a Symbol

Think about how you can find your way back to your partner from a disconnected state. We have talked about touch. In a disconnected state people tend to gravitate physically away from each other. But you might want to make up some other symbols of connection that have special meaning to the two of you. It might be a picture of the two of you together in an obviously happy, connected state. It might be a note which says "I really want to connect with you but I don't know how, help me!" It might be two special wine glasses labelled with plaques that simply state "connect please". It might be a special food like chocolate but it has the meaning between you that by offering it you are choosing to connect and by accepting it you accept the connection attempt. For men especially, admitting defeat in an argument can feel like castration to his caveman, hunter, alpha male mindset. But accepting a wineglass or something pleasurable like chocolate is an act to connect without saying anything, without admitting defeat and therefore without accepting shame.

Strategy Three – What You Do With Bids

The Gottman Institute gives great tips on relationships which are evidenced based coming from four decades of studying couples. I have referred to some of their points before. One fascinating tip they promote is what they call a bid for connection. It is simply when your partner gives an emotional sigh. That sigh, the Gottman's call a bid for connection. It might be a frustration or problem your partner is dealing with which causes them to make a sigh. In that moment, you have a choice whether to turn towards your partner, accept their bid and connect with them or turn away and ignore their bid and increase the distance between you. These are really missed opportunities if we don't turn to connect with our partners during these times. Connected couples are able to notice their partner's bids. They show interest and ask questions rather than trying to give advice and move on. By accepting a bid and turning towards your partner you are practising compassion and building connection.

One thing is absolutely certain. You will have disagreements, problems and conflicts in your relationship. These things usually isolate and polarise the couple emotionally. The skill of being able to find connection in the midst of problems and conflict in particular is probably the single most important skill in order to stay connected. The problem is that the way back after conflict is not usually stopped by the original issue. It is more often thwarted by the fighting style of the couple.

Couples who repeatedly destroy each other in conflicts as enemies have shallow, fragile relationships that are unhappy and insecure. When a problem arises, seek connection first, don't let it isolate you from your partner like a lot of people do. That's why intimacy tolerance is so important. It allows you to step into the storm of your partner's emotional environment, find them and then connect with them. No matter how huge the hurricane of the emotional sigh, you step into it and don't become all reactive making things worse. You are there to exercise compassion and to connect with them and to face the hurricane as a team. The bottom line is if you want more romance, show more compassion. Use these three strategies to help you build compassion, connection and closeness even in the more difficult times.

Compassion also means you can genuinely put yourself in the other person's position and see it from their point of view. Because we are such egocentric creatures we find it difficult to let go of our defensive position to go around to see how the "enemy" sees the fight. Even our thoughts tend to revolve around ourselves and we fall into the trap of "selfing" quite easily. But the trick is to realise that if your core vulnerability is being poked, and you are feeling insecure or anxious as a woman, or shamed as a man, then your partner is feeling their sore spot. So rather than focusing on the insecurity, bring compassion to your man's shame. If you're a man, then stop focusing on your shame and your response to fight or hide, turn and have compassion on your woman's insecurity.

Serotonin And Compassion

Serotonin is also a fascinating chemical. One of the things serotonin does is that it puts a brake on our emotions. When emotions are created at the amygdala in the bottom central part of the brain the neuron pathways carry messages to the prefrontal cortex of the brain. This is the area that is meant to be the advanced, rational part of the brain so the emotions can then be acted on sensibly and rationally. Sometimes emotions get ahead of the game and they are not screened by the prefrontal cortex and our emotions rule us instead of us ruling our emotions. When a person starts to act irrationally, we often say, "Think about it", or "Wait a minute". After a while the person cools down and takes another line of action. However, people who fall headlong into love end up with low serotonin levels. These levels tend to even themselves out after about eighteen months. Low serotonin levels usually result in greater and deeper depression and anxiety. But there is another emotion which serotonin usually puts the brakes on when it is in normal amounts. It is the emotion of obsession. Young lovers with low serotonin levels not only feel the positive emotions more deeply, they become obsessive about them. Young lovers spend most of their day fantasising about their new lover. Not helped at all by buckets of dopamine which floods in when in love, a couple in love do become obsessive with each other. It has led many researches to label that early, low serotonin stage of relationships the romantic stage which they will tell you lasts for about that first eighteen months until the serotonin levels even themselves out again.

While serotonin in normal levels acts to put the brakes on emotions it also means it puts the brakes on fight or flight emotions as well. It helps regulates negative emotions such as anger. This has led scientists to ask the questions, "What causes low serotonin levels?" and "Are some people born without those brakes on anger?" We now know that genes control the serotonin system. One of those are called the transporter gene, it regulates how much serotonin you have. In studies in monkeys it has been found that the short version of the gene means less serotonin. The long version of the gene means more serotonin. However, and this is the most interesting of all this research, monkeys that have the short version and are reared by their mother, who are nurtured and cared for don't show uncontrolled fits of anger and rage. But those with the short version who miss out on maternal nurture by being reared by peers for instance, are the ones with all the rage and aggression. From these studies scientist have concluded that nurturing helps form the serotonin pathways in the growing brain. This has huge implications for how emotions are not only experienced but how serotonin and compassion interact. Let me explain.

Erick Erickson was a psychologist who promoted a theory of psycho-social development. Without going into all the stages (you can study these easily yourself) the stage which has interest to us is the very first stage which Erickson calls the infant stage. It starts when the baby is born and ends when the baby becomes a toddler. What Erikson proposed is that a baby learns to either trust the world or mistrust the world. If the baby's mother is nurturing, has compassion on the baby and has lots of positive eye contact during this stage then the baby learns that his or her needs will be met. If he or she is changed when soiled, fed and nurtured the baby can be contented and happy. When a baby is born it's eyes can only focus a short length. It's about the distance between nipple and face. It can see the mother's expressions of acceptance and compassion. However, when a baby lacks positive interactions, has its needs not met for extended periods and misses out on the eye contact and positive facial expressions, Erikson proposes the baby decides the world can't be trusted. It then takes this mistrust with it throughout the rest of it's life. Not only is the belief of mistrust ingrained but the implication is that I must not be okay because I am not accepted. We all understand the importance of nurture for a baby. We are also aware that traumatic upbringings and abuse creates broken people. What we are probably not so aware of are the more subtle impressions on the growing brain of babies. For example, mothers who now interact more with their smart phone when feeding their babies, rather than looking at their baby, holding their gaze and sending positive messages to them. Mothers who risk others to create this bonding because they are too busy. Mothers who don't really want their babies for whatever reason, and communicate to the early child they are not wanted or needed.

The whole area of eye contact and bonding is an interesting topic. The brain waves of mothers and their babies have been measured when the baby is breastfeeding and the eye gaze between mother and baby is held. What happens is the brain waves become synced and mimic each other. The flow of positive feelings both ways takes place. How much of a role does a lack of bonding play in increasing the risk of creating personality disorders and people who lack empathy and guilt? If smart phone use while feeding a baby is detrimental, then we could start seeing a whole generation of people not only with low serotonin levels from incomplete pathways formed but also a whole generation who mistrust the world. More sociopaths and more narcissistic personality disorders? Low serotonin levels stop the regulation of emotions, so will we see more depressed, or more anxious, or angrier people than in previous generations? It has probably already started.

One last thing about serotonin. A long embrace can actually increase the serotonin levels in your body. This means that it will help with a calming influence on the huggers. If you are feeling stressed, irritable, depressed or even angry the long embrace will help soothe those negative emotions and make them feel not so intense that they are about to take over everything. Patricia Love and Steven Stosny report that practising long embraces multiple times every day also help to reduce appetite because of the increased serotonin levels it produces. They go on and comment, "Not a bad deal – you'll feel better in general and less edgy, irritable and sad in particular, and maybe drop a pound or two in the process of feeling closer."[30]

Let's return to positive bonding. If a baby is nurtured, has loving eye contact and concludes he or she can trust the world, then the baby is prepared for later socialisation and ultimately intimate relationships. It is this very early positive bonding which is so important for all of us, that deep down makes us feel nurtured when we experience compassion in our intimate relationship. When we give out compassion, it actually makes us feel good. But when we are recipients of compassion it makes us feel good because it reminds us of our decision to trust. It reminds us that we are in fact okay. It reminds us that we are loved and adored. Is it any wonder then that deep kissing which replicates the action of sucking at our mother's breast, is so bonding, and so enjoyable? The bottom line is that compassion during infancy is so important. But compassion during intimacy, and between loving partners generally is a familiar reminder that we can trust, lower our defences and be vulnerable, so we can go deeper pleasurably with our partner. Turn the compassion button on, and watch romance flourish.

Several years ago I was presenting a series of relationship seminars. One woman came up to me after a few weeks and said how there was one point (only one I was thinking?) that really stuck with her. I had made the statement, "If you want the best spouse in your relationship, be the best spouse." She said she had gone home and given this a lot of thought. She said she had been so focused on wanting to change her husband that she had completely missed her responsibility and the one thing she had the power to change, herself. She started focusing her energy on being the best spouse. She started practising compassion and connection. She soon forgot the things she wanted to change in her husband. But as her husband became connected with her again he started reciprocating what she had begun. It wasn't very long before he wanted to become the best spouse as well.

> *"If you want the best spouse in your relationship, be the best spouse."*

Years ago I was called to a man who wanted to take his own life. I was working with a female paramedic at the time who I had a great amount of respect for. She had a great way with patients regardless of what situation they were in. This patient who was suicidal and serious in his intentions listened to my partner who was trying to get through to him. In the course of the conversation she made the statement, "Death comes soon enough mate, you don't want to hurry it up!" The patient responded positively to it and agreed. I have thought about her statement many times over the years since. She is so right. Death is coming to us all way too quickly, the last thing you need to do is to speed it up! If you are going to live for this short speck of time on this tiny planet of ours which is in itself a tiny speck in the universe why not live your life as meaningfully as possible. Why not turn that darn romance button on and enjoy wherever it takes you whatever the consequences because the end of the line comes far sooner than we all realise.

Building Intimacy In Your Relationship

Distraction is a major problem in today's relationships. We are continually being over-stimulated by electronic devices that crowd out intimacy. Here are some ideas on building intimacy and increasing intimacy tolerance for both partners. The first one is to put away all distractions and look into each other's eyes for a minimum of five minutes without breaking gaze. Sit opposite each other and have a gap of only 60 centimetres. After the five minutes has expired, talk to each other about what you felt, what you were thinking during the exercise and if you discovered anything new.

The second one is to relax in a comfortable setting and listen to a minimum of five of your favourite love songs and five of your partner's favourite love songs. Lay together and tenderly caress and touch each other, rub your partner's shoulders or if they have long hair, brush it.

The third one comes from The New York Times which once listed 36 questions you can ask someone if you want to fall in love or make love even stronger. Check out 36questionsinlove.com and go through the questions with your partner. Don't rush them but allow yourselves time to ponder them and listen to what each other has to say instead of preparing in your mind your own responses while your mate is talking.

The fourth one is to sing a love song to your partner while looking into their eyes. You can sing along with a recording, sing without music or write your own lyrics to existing music but it must be a love song.

The fifth one is to both make a list of ten things you are both thankful for in your partner. Then you both get to read out the lists slowly to each other.

The sixth one is to go somewhere public with the express purpose to engage in public displays of affection.

The seventh one is to go and visit a hospice together and talk with someone who is dying. Get into a deep and meaningful conversation rather than limiting yourself to a shallow topic. Go home and talk together about your experience.

The eighth one is to volunteer together your time helping someone else. Volunteer your time at a soup kitchen, a homeless shelter or hospital. Go home and talk about your reactions and thoughts.

The ninth one is to sit down with a hot drink and discuss what your dreams are. What do you want to do together? What's your bucket list? Where is the one place more than anywhere else you wish to go before you die?

Finally, stand face to face with your partner. Look them in the eyes for one minute. Then cup their face in your hands and deep kiss them for one minute. Then walk around behind them and spoon them standing up, cuddling them from behind for one more minute. Slowly kiss the nape of their neck for one more minute. Then move around to the front again and hug your partner trying to get as much body to body contact as possible and then hold for one minute. Then swap roles with your partner so your partner then copies what you have just done for the same lengths of time. When you are comfortable with this one you can go to an advanced version. Follow the same procedure only the first person who is in the passive role, the one that is being kissed initially that is, takes their clothes off so they are completely naked while the other is fully dressed. Then it becomes the other's turn as roles are swapped. Discuss your experiences and how you felt, what you found the most threatening and which role you found more exciting. The answer may surprise you. Then you can complete the whole exercise again with both of you fully naked.

Building intimacy can be challenging and may push both partners past their comfort zones. But remember that anxiety has the same features as excitement. Everyday people push their boundaries to experience exhilaration. They go to theme parks, ride roller coasters, jump out of planes and generally scare the living daylights out of themselves all to get an exciting rush of neurological chemicals surging into their bodies. Deep romantic connection is very similar. It involves giving up control somewhat. It involves throwing your exposed, naked self at another human being and taking the chance to see if they will accept you just as you really are. But when they do accept you and throw themselves at you to do the same it can be just as exhilarating. You have the chance to intimately bond with another living person who has a mind of their own, is very different from you and will be at times very unpredictable. You are invited to trust, to love and to cherish this other special human being and give of yourself totally with the opportunity to connect with and protect this person like no one else on the planet. How much you commit of yourself is up to you. How much you hold back of yourself is also your choice. But if you go in all out, you are set for an amazing adventure of discovery mixed with self-discovery, with excitement mixed with fear but with depth and meaning revealing itself each day. Romance, turn the button to on. No stuff it. Jam that button to fully on and break it off in that position and then sit back and enjoy the ride. It's going to be breath taking!

SUMMARY OF CHAPTER ELEVEN

Modern day Caveman Characteristics

Confidence (men like it, women are drawn to it)
Opposite is shame – it activates cortisol
Harsh start up activates cortisol/shame
Solution – use soft start up

Communication differences
Conversations about the relationship activates shame in men
Solution – Touch first and freely
Touch stimulates oxytocin which bonds a couple
Connect first before any speech

Strength
The challenge is to make her feel safe in the relationship
Any fear a woman has should be re-framed as a request for protection
Solution – Protection invites compassion

Science reveals compassion has many benefits

Compassion must replace cortisol if we want a romantic, connected relationship

"Selfing" and mind wandering add to stress responses and distract a couple from connecting

Practise connecting and protecting so it becomes automatic and natural

During difficult times:

Focus on commitment

Practise fighting/reconnecting

Practise finding your way back to your partner so you become really good at it

Create personal symbols of reconnecting

Build intimacy and increase intimacy tolerance by following the exercises

Jam the romance button to on!

Author's Note

I hope you've enjoyed this book and you endorse the benefits of romance in your relationship. If you have, I would kindly ask you to please leave a review of the book on the site where you purchased it. Even just one paragraph helps others decide if it might be the book for them. And what better way than to hear from an objective person who has just finished reading the book! You might find it helpful to review the chapter summaries to remember what parts you found the most helpful, inspiring or thought provoking. Furthermore, if you want to contact me, follow me or check out my blogs you can do so at romanceisalive.com or facebook.com/relationshipsplus. You can also check out my author page on Amazon which is linked to the book. I wish you all the very best romance has to offer.

12

References

1. ^ Adapted from *why am I afraid to tell you who I am?* By John Powell (Argus Communications, Texas; 1969) pages 50 to 69
2. ^ *The Language of Sex From A to Z World Almanac*, by Kenneth N. Anderson and Robert M. Goldenson (Bloomsbury Publishing, London, 1986) page 216.
3. ^ *What Wives Wish Their Husbands Knew About Women*, by Dr. James Dobson (Tyndale House Publishers, Inc., Wheaton, Illinios. 1975) page 65.
4. ^ *How To Keep A Man In Love With You Forever*, by Tracy Cabot (Columbus Books, London, 1987) page 245 - 246.
5. ^ Dobson James, op.cit., page 64 - 65.
6. ^ *Why Men Are The Way They Are*, by Warren Farell (McGraw-Hill, New York, 1986) page 20.
7. ^ *The Romance Factor*, by Allan Loy McGinnis (Harper & Row Publishers, San Francisco 1982) page 5.
8. ^ Farrell, Warren, op cit., page 330.
9. ^ Ibid, page 331
10. ^ Ibid, page 331
11. ^ Cabot Tracy, op. cit., page 127.

12. ^ *Solomon On Sex* By Joseph Dillow (Thomas Nelson Publishers, Nashville Tennessee 1977) page 27
13. ^*Treating Sexual Disorders* Ed. R Charlton (Jossey-Bass, San Francisco, 1997) page 246
14. ^DSM-IV-TR Diagnostic and Statistical Manual of Mental Disorders (Washington DC American Psychiatric Association 2000) page 539
15. ^ *Good Loving Great Sex* By Dr Rosie King (Random House Milson's Point 1998) page 147
16. ^ *Treating Sexual Disorders* Ed. R. Charlton (Jossey-Bass, San Francisco;1997) p 218
17. ^ See Professor Lorraine Dennerstein's work as summarised by menopause.org.au (article titled *Libido and the natural menopause transition*)
18. ^ See the aafp.org (American Academy of Family Physicians) website for in depth articles related to the treatment of HSDD in women.
19. ^ Kingsberg SA, Clayton AH, Pfaus JG. *The female sexual response: current models, neurobiological underpinnings and agents currently approved or under investigation for the treatment of hypoactive sexual desire disorder.* CNS Drugs, 2015; 29(II): 915-933
20. ^ See Mayo Clinic Consensus recommendations - Hypoactive Sexual Desire Disorder: International Society for the Study of Women's Sexual Health (ISSWSH) Expert Consensus Panel Review
21. ^ See Professor Lorraine Dennerstein's work as summarised by menopause.org.au (article titled *Libido and the natural menopause transition*)
22. ^ *How To Dramatically Increase Your Wife's Sex Drive*, by Paul Gaughan (Austed Publishing Company, O'Connor, 1992) page 45.

23. ^ Score sheet adapted from *The Relaxation & Stress Reduction Workbook* 5th Edition By Martha Davis Ph.D., Elizabeth Robbins Eshelman, M.S.W, Matthew McKay, Ph.D. (New Harbinger Publications, Inc. 2000) pages 110-114
24. ^ Farrell, Warren op. cit., page 332.
25. ^ *The Compleat Marriage*, by Nancy Van Pelt, (Southern Publishing Association, Nashville, Tennessee,1976) page 47.
26. ^ *Beyond Mateship*, by Terry Colling. (East Roseville, Simon & Schuster, Australia 1992) page 67.
27. ^ *Why Women Talk and Men Walk* How to improve Your Relationship without Discussing it (Vermilion, London 2007) page 10
28. ^ See Dr Elissa Epel Youtubes on her work with mindfulness, compassion and stress reduction.
29. ^Loving-Kindness Meditation practice associated with longer telomeres in women By Elizabeth Hoge and seven others (Sciencedirect.com)
30. ^ *Why Women Talk and Men Walk* How to improve Your Relationship without Discussing it, By Patrica Love and Steven Stonsy (Vermilion, London, 2007) page 202

www.ingramcontent.com/pod-product-compliance
Lightning Source LLC
Chambersburg PA
CBHW070249010526
44107CB00056B/2400